Informing the legislative debate since 1914 _____

Navy Ford (CVN-78) Class Aircraft Carrier Program: Background and Issues for Congress

Ronald O'Rourke

Specialist in Naval Affairs

June 4, 2014

Congressional Research Service

7-5700

www.crs.gov

RS20643

CRS REPORT
Prepared for Members and
Committees of Congress _____

Summary

CVN-78, CVN-79, and CVN-80 are the first three ships in the Navy's new Gerald R. Ford (CVN-78) class of nuclear-powered aircraft carriers (CVNs).

CVN-78 was procured in FY2008. The Navy's proposed FY2015 budget estimates the ship's procurement cost at $12,887.2 million (i.e., about $12.9 billion) in then-year dollars. The ship received advance procurement funding in FY2001-FY2007 and was fully funded in FY2008-FY2011 using congressionally authorized four-year incremental funding. The Navy did not request any procurement funding for the ship in FY2012 and FY2013. To help cover cost growth on the ship, the ship received an additional $588.1 million in procurement funding in FY2014, and the Navy is requesting another $663.0 million in procurement funding for FY2015.

CVN-79 was procured in FY2013. The ship received advance procurement funding in FY2007-FY2012, and the Navy plans to fully fund the ship in FY2013-FY2018 using congressionally authorized six-year incremental funding. The Navy's proposed FY2015 budget estimates CVN-79's procurement cost at $11,498.0 million (i.e., about $11.5 billion) in then-year dollars, and requests $1,300 million in procurement funding for the ship.

CVN-80 is scheduled to be procured in FY2018. The Navy's proposed FY2015 budget estimates the ship's procurement cost at $13,874.2 million (i.e., about $13.9 billion) in then-year dollars. Under the Navy's proposed FY2015 budget, the ship is to receive advance procurement funding in FY2016-FY2017 and be fully funded in FY2018-FY2023 using congressionally authorized six-year incremental funding.

Oversight issues for Congress for the CVN-78 program include the following:

- cost growth in the CVN-78 program;

- CVN-78 program issues that were raised in a January 2014 report from the Department of Defense's (DOD's) Director of Operational Test and Evaluation (DOT&E); and

- the potential for a two-ship block buy on CVN-79 and CVN-80.

An additional issue relating to aircraft carriers that has been raised by the Navy's proposed FY2015 budget concerns funding for the mid-life nuclear refueling overhaul of the aircraft carrier *George Washington* (CVN-73).

Contents

Figures

Tables

Appendixes

Contacts

Introduction

This report provides background information and potential oversight issues for Congress on the Gerald R. Ford (CVN-78) class aircraft carrier program. Congress's decisions on the CVN-78 program could substantially affect Navy capabilities and funding requirements and the shipbuilding industrial base.

An additional issue relating to aircraft carriers that has been raised by the Navy's proposed FY2015 budget concerns funding for the mid-life nuclear refueling overhaul of the aircraft carrier *George Washington* (CVN-73). This issue is discussed in **Appendix B**.

Background

The Navy's Aircraft Carrier Force

The Navy's current aircraft carrier force consists of 10 nuclear-powered Nimitz-class ships (CVNs 68 through 77) that entered service between 1975 and 2009. Until December 2012, the Navy's aircraft carrier force included an 11th aircraft carrier—the one-of-a-kind nuclear-powered *Enterprise* (CVN-65), which entered service in 1961. CVN-65 was inactivated on December 1, 2012, reducing the Navy's carrier force from 11 ships to 10. The most recently commissioned carrier, *George H. W. Bush* (CVN-77), the final Nimitz-class ship, was procured in FY2001 and commissioned into service on January 10, 2009. CVN-77 replaced *Kitty Hawk* (CV-63), which was the Navy's last remaining conventionally powered carrier.[1]

Statutory Requirement to Maintain Not Less Than 11 Carriers

Origin of Requirement

10 U.S.C. 5062(b) requires the Navy to maintain a force of not less than 11 operational aircraft carriers. The requirement for the Navy to maintain not less than a certain number of operational aircraft carriers was established by Section 126 of the FY2006 National Defense Authorization Act (H.R. 1815/P.L. 109-163 of January 6, 2006), which set the number at 12 carriers. The requirement was changed from 12 carriers to 11 carriers by Section 1011(a) of the FY2007 John Warner National Defense Authorization Act (H.R. 5122/P.L. 109-364 of October 17, 2006).

Waiver for Period Between CVN-65 and CVN-78

As mentioned above, the carrier force dropped from 11 ships to 10 ships when *Enterprise* (CVN-65) was inactivated on December 1, 2012. The carrier force is to return to 11 ships when its replacement, *Gerald R. Ford* (CVN-78), is commissioned into service. CVN-78 was originally scheduled to be delivered in September 2015, but its construction has been running behind schedule, and the Navy in May 2013 announced that the ship's delivery date had been postponed

---

[1] The *Kitty Hawk* was decommissioned on January 31, 2009.

to February 2016.[2] The Navy's FY2015 budget submission shows a delivery date of March 2016. Anticipating the gap between the inactivation of CVN-65 and the commissioning of CVN-78, the Navy asked Congress for a temporary waiver of 10 U.S.C. 5062(b) to accommodate the period between the two events. Section 1023 of the FY2010 National Defense Authorization Act (H.R. 2647/P.L. 111-84 of October 28, 2009) authorized the waiver, permitting the Navy to have 10 operational carriers between the inactivation of CVN-65 and the commissioning of CVN-78.

Funding and Procuring Aircraft Carriers

Some Key Terms

The Navy *procures* a ship (i.e., orders the ship) by awarding a full-ship construction contract to the firm building the ship.

Part of a ship's procurement cost might be provided through *advance procurement (AP) funding*. AP funding is funding provided in one or more years prior to (i.e., in advance of) a ship's year of procurement. AP funding is used to pay for long-leadtime components that must be ordered ahead of time to ensure that they will be ready in time for their scheduled installation into the ship. AP funding is also used to pay for the design costs for a new class of ship. These design costs, known more formally as *detailed design/non-recurring engineering (DD/NRE) costs*, are traditionally incorporated into the procurement cost of the lead ship in a new class of ships.

Fully funding a ship means funding the entire procurement cost of the ship. If a ship has received AP funding, then fully funding the ship means paying for the remaining portion of the ship's procurement cost.

The *full funding policy* is a Department of Defense (DOD) policy that normally requires items acquired through the procurement title of the annual DOD appropriations act to be fully funded in the year they are procured. In recent years, Congress has authorized DOD to use *incremental funding* for procuring certain Navy ships, most notably aircraft carriers. Under incremental funding, some of the funding needed to fully fund a ship is provided in one or more years after the year in which the ship is procured.[3]

Incremental Funding Authority for Aircraft Carriers

Section 121 of the FY2007 John Warner National Defense Authorization Act (H.R. 5122/P.L. 109-364 of October 17, 2006) granted the Navy the authority to use four-year incremental funding for CVNs 78, 79, and 80. Under this authority, the Navy could fully fund each of these ships over a four-year period that includes the ship's year of procurement and three subsequent years.

---

[2] *Report to Congress on the Annual Long-Range Plan for Construction of Naval Vessels for FY2014*, May 2013, p. 13.

[3] For more on full funding, incremental funding, and AP funding, see CRS Report RL31404, *Defense Procurement: Full Funding Policy—Background, Issues, and Options for Congress*, by Ronald O'Rourke and Stephen Daggett, and CRS Report RL32776, *Navy Ship Procurement: Alternative Funding Approaches—Background and Options for Congress*, by Ronald O'Rourke.

Section 124 of the FY2012 National Defense Authorization Act (H.R. 1540/P.L. 112-81 of December 31, 2011) amended Section 121 of P.L. 109-364 to grant the Navy the authority to use five-year incremental funding for CVNs 78, 79, and 80. Since CVN-78 was fully funded in FY2008-FY2011, the provision in practice applied to CVNs 79 and 80.

Section 121 of the FY2013 National Defense Authorization Act (H.R. 4310/P.L. 112-239 of January 2, 2013) amended Section 121 of P.L. 109-364 to grant the Navy the authority to use six-year incremental funding for CVNs 78, 79, and 80. Since CVN-78 was fully funded in FY2008-FY2011, the provision in practice applies to CVNs 79 and 80.

Aircraft Carrier Construction Industrial Base

All U.S. aircraft carriers procured since FY1958 have been built by Newport News Shipbuilding (NNS), of Newport News, VA, a shipyard that is part of Huntington Ingalls Industries (HII). NNS is the only U.S. shipyard that can build large-deck, nuclear-powered aircraft carriers. The aircraft carrier construction industrial base also includes hundreds of subcontractors and suppliers in various states.

Gerald R. Ford (CVN-78) Class Program

The Gerald R. Ford (CVN-78) class carrier design (**Figure 1**) is the successor to the Nimitz-class carrier design.[4]

---

[4] The CVN-78 class was earlier known as the CVN-21 class, which meant nuclear-powered aircraft carrier for the 21st century.

Figure 1. Navy Illustration of CVN-78

Source: Navy image accessed at http://www.navy.mil/management/photodb/photos/060630-N-0000X-001.jpg on April 20, 2011.

The Ford-class design uses the basic Nimitz-class hull form but incorporates several improvements, including features permitting the ship to generate about 25% more aircraft sorties per day, more electrical power for supporting ship systems, and features permitting the ship to be operated by several hundred fewer sailors than a Nimitz-class ship, significantly reducing life-cycle operating and support (O&S) costs.

Navy plans call for procuring at least three Ford-class carriers—CVN-78, CVN-79, and CVN-80.

CVN-78

CVN-78, which was named for President Gerald R. Ford in 2007,[5] was procured in FY2008. The Navy's proposed FY2015 budget estimates the ship's procurement cost at $12,887.2 million (i.e., about $12.9 billion) in then-year dollars. Of the ship's total procurement cost, about $3.3 billion is for detailed design/non-recurring engineering (DD/NRE) costs for the class, and about $9.6 billion is for construction of the ship itself.

---

[5] §1012 of the FY2007 defense authorization act (H.R. 5122/P.L. 109-364 of October 17, 2006) expressed the sense of the Congress that CVN-78 should be named for President Gerald R. Ford. On January 16, 2007, the Navy announced that CVN-78 would be so named. CVN-78 and other carriers built to the same design will consequently be referred to as Ford (CVN-78) class carriers. For more on Navy ship names, see CRS Report RS22478, *Navy Ship Names: Background for Congress*, by Ronald O'Rourke.

CVN-78 received advance procurement funding in FY2001-FY2007 and was fully funded in FY2008-FY2011 using congressionally authorized four-year incremental funding. The Navy did not request any procurement funding for the ship in FY2012 and FY2013. To help cover cost growth on the ship, the ship received an additional $588.1 million in procurement funding in FY2014, and the Navy is requesting another $663.0 million in procurement funding for FY2015.

CVN-79

CVN-79, which was named for President John F. Kennedy on May 29, 2011,[6] was procured in FY2013. The ship received advance procurement funding in FY2007-FY2012, and the Navy plans to fully fund the ship in FY2013-FY2018 using congressionally authorized six-year incremental funding. The Navy's proposed FY2015 budget estimates CVN-79's procurement cost at $11,498.0 million (i.e., about $11.5 billion) in then-year dollars, and requests $1,300 million in procurement funding for the ship.

CVN-80

CVN-80, which was named *Enterprise* on December 1, 2012,[7] is scheduled to be procured in FY2018. The Navy's proposed FY2014 budget estimates the ship's procurement cost at $13,874.2 million (i.e., about $13.9 billion) in then-year dollars. Under the Navy's proposed FY2015 budget, the ship is to receive advance procurement funding in FY2016-FY2017 and be fully funded in FY2018-FY2023 using congressionally authorized six-year incremental funding.

Program Procurement Funding

Table 1 shows procurement funding for CVNs 78, 79, and 80 through FY2018.

---

[6] See "Navy Names Next Aircraft Carrier USS John F. Kennedy," *Navy News Service*, May 29, 2011, accessed online on June 1, 2011 at http://www.navy.mil/search/display.asp?story_id=60686. See also Peter Frost, "U.S. Navy's Next Aircraft Carrier Will Be Named After The Late John F. Kennedy," *Newport News Daily Press*, May 30, 2011. CVN-79 is the second ship to be named for President John F. Kennedy. The first, CV-67, was the last conventionally powered carrier procured for the Navy. CV-67 was procured in FY1963, entered service in 1968, and was decommissioned in 2007.

[7] The Navy made the announcement of CVN-80's name on the same day that it deactivated the 51-year-old aircraft carrier CVN-65, also named *Enterprise*. ("Enterprise, Navy's First Nuclear-Powered Aircraft Carrier, Inactivated," *Navy News Service*, December 1, 2012; Hugh Lessig, "Navy Retires One Enterprise, Will Welcome Another," *Newport News Daily Press*, December 2, 2012.) CVN-65 was the eighth Navy ship named *Enterprise*; CVN-80 is to be the ninth.

Table 1. Procurement Funding for CVNs 78, 79, and 80 Through FY2019

(Millions of then-year dollars, rounded to nearest tenth)

FY	CVN-78	CVN-79	CVN-80	Total
FY01	21.7 (AP)	0	0	21.7
FY02	135.3 (AP)	0	0	135.3
FY03	395.5 (AP)	0	0	395.5
FY04	1,162.9 (AP)	0	0	1,162.9
FY05	623.1 (AP)	0	0	623.1
FY06	618.9 (AP)	0	0	618.9
FY07	735.8 (AP)	52.8 (AP)	0	788.6
FY08	2,685.0 (FF)	123.5 (AP)	0	2,808.6
FY09	2,684.6 (FF)	1,210.6 (AP)	0	3,895.1
FY10	737.0 (FF)	482.9 (AP)	0	1,219.9
FY11	1,712.5 (FF)	903.3 (AP)	0	2,615.8
FY12	0	554.8 (AP)	0	554.8
FY13	0	491.0 (FF)	0	491.0
FY14	588.1 (CC)	917.6 (FF)	0	1,505.7
FY15 (requested)	*663.0 (CC)*	*1,300.0 (FF)*	*0*	*1,963.0*
FY16 (projected)	*124.0 (CC)*	*2,193.0 (FF)*	*683.2 (AP)*	*3,000.2*
FY17 (projected)	*0*	*1,245.6 (FF)*	*1,045.2 (AP)*	*2,290.8*
FY18 (projected)	*0*	*2,023.8 (FF)*	*825.5 (FF)*	*2,849.3*
FY19 (projected)	*0*	*0*	*1,864.5 (FF)*	*1,864.5*

Source: Table prepared by CRS based on FY2009-FY2015 Navy budget submissions.

Notes: Figures may not add due to rounding. "AP" is advance procurement funding; "FF" is full funding; "CC" is cost to complete funding (i.e., funding to cover cost growth).

Increases in Estimated Unit Procurement Costs Since FY2008 Budget

Table 2 shows changes in the estimated procurement costs of CVNs 78, 79, and 80 since the FY2008 budget submission.[8]

---

[8] CBO in 2008 and the Government Accountability Office (GAO) in 2007 questioned the accuracy of the Navy's cost estimate for CVN-78. CBO reported in June 2008 that it estimated that CVN-78 would cost $11.2 billion in constant FY2009 dollars, or about $900 million more than the Navy's estimate of $10.3 billion in constant FY2009 dollars, and that if "CVN-78 experienced cost growth similar to that of other lead ships that the Navy has purchased in the past 10 years, costs could be much higher still." CBO also reported that, although the Navy publicly expressed confidence in its cost estimate for CVN-78, the Navy had assigned a confidence level of less than 50% to its estimate, meaning that the Navy believed there was more than a 50% chance that the estimate would be exceeded. (Congressional Budget Office, *Resource Implications of the Navy's Fiscal Year 2009 Shipbuilding Plan*, June 9, 2008, p. 20.) GAO reported in August 2007 that:

> Costs for CVN 78 will likely exceed the budget for several reasons. First, the Navy's cost estimate, which underpins the budget, is optimistic. For example, the Navy assumes that CVN 78 will be built with fewer labor hours than were needed for the previous two carriers. Second, the Navy's target cost for ship construction may not be achievable. The shipbuilder's initial cost estimate for construction was 22 percent higher than the Navy's cost target, which was based on the budget. Although the Navy and the shipbuilder are working on ways to reduce costs, the actual costs to build the ship will likely increase above the Navy's target. Third, the Navy's ability to manage issues that affect cost suffers from insufficient cost surveillance. Without effective cost

(continued...)

Table 2. Changes in Estimated Procurement Costs of CVNs 78, 79, and 80

(As shown in FY2008-FY2015 budgets, in millions of then-year dollars)

Budget	CVN-78		CVN-79		CVN-80	
	Estimated procurement cost	Scheduled fiscal year of procurement	Estimated procurement cost	Scheduled fiscal year of procurement	Estimated procurement cost	Scheduled fiscal year of procurement
FY08 budget	10,488.9	FY08	9,192.0	FY12	10,716.8	FY16
FY09 budget	10,457.9	FY08	9,191.6	FY12	10,716.8	FY16
FY10 budget	10,845.8	FY08	n/a[a]	FY13[b]	n/a[a]	FY18[b]
FY11 budget	11,531.0	FY08	10,413.1	FY13	13,577.0	FY18
FY12 budget	11,531.0	FY08	10,253.0	FY13	13,494.9	FY18
FY13 budget	12,323.2	FY08	11,411.0	FY13[c]	13,874.2	FY18[c]
FY14 budget	12,829.3	FY08	11,338.4	FY13	13,874.2	FY18
FY15 budget	12,887.2	FY08	11,498.0	FY13	13,874.2	FY18
% change:						
FY08 budget to FY09 budget	-0.3		Almost no change		No change	
FY09 budget to FY10 budget	+3.7		n/a		n/a	
FY10 budget to FY11 budget	+6.3		n/a		n/a	
FY11 budget to FY12 budget	No change		- 1.5		- 0.1	
FY12 budget to FY13 budget	+6.9%		+11.3%		+2.8%	
FY13 budget to FY14 budget	+4.1%		- 0.6%		No change	
FY14 budget to FY15 budget	+0.5%		+1.4%		No change	
FY08 budget to FY15 budget	+22.9%		+25.1%		+29.5%	

Source: Table prepared by CRS based on FY2008-FY2015 Navy budget submissions.

a. n/a means not available; the FY2010 budget submission did not show estimated procurement costs for CVNs 79 and 80.

b. The FY2010 budget submission did not show scheduled years of procurement for CVNs 79 and 80; the dates shown here for the FY2010 budget submission are inferred from the shift to five-year intervals for procuring carriers that was announced by Secretary of Defense Gates in his April 6, 2009, news conference regarding recommendations for the FY2010 defense budget.

(...continued)

surveillance, the Navy will not be able to identify early signs of cost growth and take necessary corrective action.

(Government Accountability Office, Defense Acquisitions[:] Navy Faces Challenges Constructing the Aircraft Carrier Gerald R. Ford within Budget, GAO-07-866, August 2007, summary page. See also Government Accountability Office, Defense Acquisitions[:] Realistic Business Cases Needed to Execute Navy Shipbuilding Programs, Statement of Paul L. Francis, Director, Acquisition and Sourcing Management Team, Testimony Before the Subcommittee on Seapower and Expeditionary Forces, Committee on Armed Services, House of Representatives, July 24, 2007 (GAO-07-943T), p. 15.)

    c.   Although the FY2013 budget did not change the scheduled years of procurement for CVN-79 and CVN-80 compared to what they were under the FY2012 budget, it lengthened the construction period for each ship by two years (i.e., each ship is scheduled to be delivered two years later than under the FY2012 budget).

Program Procurement Cost Cap

Section 122 of the FY2007 John Warner National Defense Authorization Act (H.R. 5122/P.L. 109-364 of October 17, 2006) established a procurement cost cap for CVN-78 of $10.5 billion, plus adjustments for inflation and other factors, and a procurement cost cap for subsequent Ford-class carriers of $8.1 billion each, plus adjustments for inflation and other factors. The conference report (H.Rept. 109-702 of September 29, 2006) on P.L. 109-364 discusses Section 122 on pages 551-552.

Section 121 of the FY2014 National Defense Authorization Act (H.R. 3304/P.L. 113-66 of December 26, 2013) amended the procurement cost cap for the CVN-78 program to provide a revised cap of $12,887.0 million for CVN-78 and a revised cap of $11,498.0 million for each follow-on ship in the program, plus adjustments for inflation and other factors (including an additional factor not included in original cost cap).

Issues for Congress

Cost Growth

Overview

Cost growth has been a continuing oversight issue for Congress on the CVN-78 program. As shown in **Table 2**, the estimated procurement costs of CVNs 78 and 79 have grown 22.9% and 25.1%, respectively, since the submission of the FY2008 budget. As also shown in the table, CVNs 78, 79, and 80 experienced little or no cost growth from the FY2014 budget to the FY2015 budget. As shown in **Table 1**, cost growth on CVN-78 has prompted the Navy to program $1,375.1 million in additional cost-to-complete procurement funding for the ship in FY2014-FY2016.

Section 121 of the FY2014 National Defense Authorization Act (H.R. 3304/P.L. 113-66 of December 26, 2013), in addition to amending the procurement cost cap for the CVN-78 program (see previous section), requires the Navy to submit

> on a quarterly basis a report setting forth the most current cost estimate for the aircraft carrier designated as CVN-79 (as estimated by the program manager). Each cost estimate shall include the current percentage of completion of the program, the total costs incurred, and an estimate of costs at completion for ship construction, Government-furnished equipment, and engineering and support costs.

Section 121 also states that

> The Secretary [of the Navy] shall ensure that each prime contract for the aircraft carrier designated as CVN-79 includes an incentive fee structure that will, throughout the period of performance of the contract, provide incentives for each contractor to meet the portion of the cost of the ship, as limited by subsection (a)(2) and adjusted pursuant to subsection (b) [i.e.,

the amended procurement cost cap for the program], for which the contractor is responsible.'.

Navy officials have stated that they are working to control the cost of CVN-79 using a build strategy for the ship that incorporates improvements over the build strategy that was used for CVN-78. These improvements, Navy officials have said, include the following items, among others:

- achieving a higher percentage of outfitting of ship modules before modules are stacked together to form the ship;

- achieving "learning inside the ship," which means producing similar-looking ship modules in an assembly line-like series, so as to achieve improved production learning curve benefits in the production of these modules; and

- more economical ordering of parts and materials including greater use of batch ordering of parts and materials, as opposed to ordering parts and materials on an individual basis as each is needed.

The following sections present discussions of the cost growth issue from the Department of Defense (DOD), the Navy, the Congressional Budget Office (CBO), and the Government Accountability Office (GAO).

March 2014 GAO Report

A March 2014 GAO report assessing major DOD weapon acquisition programs stated the following regarding the status of the CVN-78 program, including the potential for cost growth:

Technology Maturity

According to the Navy, 7 of the 13 critical technologies for CVN 78 are mature, and the remaining 6 are approaching maturity. To meet required installation dates aboard CVN 78, the Navy produced several of these technologies, such as the volume search radar (VSR), prior to demonstrating their maturity—a strategy GAO's prior work has shown introduces risk of late and costly design changes and rework. The VSR is a component of the dual band radar (DBR), which has been delivered to CVN 78, and is undergoing design modifications needed to complete shipboard integration. According to the Navy, testing in the spring of 2015 will show whether these modifications were successful or a more extensive redesign of the system is required, which could delay DBR deliveries by up to 4 years. Deficiencies affecting water twister components—used to absorb energy when arresting aircraft—of the advanced arresting gear (AAG) technology continue to disrupt the system's development. Recent water twister redesign proved unsuccessful in testing last year. The Navy resolved problems with the redesign and is planning for concurrent testing. Despite these steps, the Navy forecasts AAG land-based testing to be complete in August 2016—a new delay of nearly two years—and after the Navy has accepted CVN 78 delivery. The electromagnetic aircraft launch system (EMALS) has successfully launched aircraft during land-based testing using a single launcher and four motor generators. The shipboard system will employ a more complex configuration with more launchers and generators sharing a power interface.

Design Maturity

CVN 78 completed its 3D product model in November 2009—over a year after the construction contract award. While the model is now considered functionally complete, maintaining design stability depends on technologies fitting within the space, weight, cooling, and power reservations allotted them. Shipboard testing may reveal a need for design changes. Also, as construction progresses, the shipbuilder is discovering "first-of-class" type design changes, which it is using to update the model prior to CVN 79 construction.

Production Maturity

According to program officials, CVN 78 is approximately 70 percent complete. Lead ship procurement costs for the lead ship have grown by over 22 percent since construction authorization in fiscal year 2008 due in part to problems encountered in construction. Out-of-sequence work driven largely by material shortfalls, engineering challenges, and delays developing and installing certain critical technologies the Navy provides to the shipbuilder for installation has affected construction progress.

Other Program Issues

The Navy deferred award of the CVN 79 detail design and construction contract from late fiscal year 2013 to the first quarter of fiscal year 2015. According to the Navy, continuing contract negotiations provide an opportunity to incorporate process improvements into construction plans. The Navy has undertaken an in-depth review of CVN 79 requirements and capabilities to identify cost trades, which it hopes can facilitate an agreement on contract terms. These actions are consistent with recommendations we made in September 2013 to defer the CVN 79 construction contract and to conduct a cost-benefit analysis on Ford-class capability requirements and the time and money needed to field systems to provide these capabilities.

Program Office Comments

According to the program office, CVN 78 displaced 77,000 tons and was 70 percent complete at launch—the highest levels achieved in aircraft carrier new construction. The program office also reported that labor inefficiencies during ship erection are past and the principal risk remaining is in shipboard testing. Concerns over system integration within platform space, weight, and power reservations have been resolved. Land based testing for EMALS and DBR has progressed enough that program officials do not anticipate significant redesign. Further, the AAG test schedule remains on track to support ship delivery and sea trials. Lastly, the Navy plans to modify the CVN 79 construction preparation contract to extend the terms of the contract and avoid a production break during negotiations on the detail design and construction contract without delaying ship delivery. Program officials also provided technical comments that were incorporated where deemed appropriate.[9]

October 2013 CBO Report

An October 2013 CBO report on the potential cost of the Navy's FY2014 30-year shipbuilding plan states:

> The Navy currently projects that the cost of the lead ship of the CVN-78 class will be $12.8 billion in nominal dollars (which is just below the new Congressional cost cap of $12.9 billion.) Using the Navy's inflation index for naval shipbuilding, CBO converted that figure to $13.9 billion in 2013 dollars. That amount is 22 percent more than the President's budget

---

[9] Government Accountability Office, *Defense Acquisitions[:] Assessments of Selected Weapon Programs*, GAO-14-340SP, March 2014, p. 74.

requested in 2008 when the ship was authorized. The Navy's estimate does not include $4.7 billion in research and development costs that apply to the entire class. In its 2014 budget request, the Navy requested an extra $506 million in nominal dollars in 2014 and 2015 ($483 million in 2013 dollars) to cover additional cost growth and additional tooling and vendor services; that amount is included in the Navy's estimate.

CBO estimates that the cost of the lead ship of the CVN-78 class will be $13.5 billion in nominal dollars and $14.5 billion in 2013 dollars. To generate that estimate, CBO used the actual costs of the previous carrier—the CVN-77—and adjusted them for the higher costs of government-furnished equipment and for more than $3 billion in costs for nonrecurring engineering and detail design (the plans, drawings, and other one-time items associated with the first ship of a new class). Subsequent ships of the CVN-78 class will not require as much funding for one-time items, although they will incur the same costs for government-furnished equipment. Altogether, CBO estimates the average cost of the 6 carriers in the 2014 plan at $12.7 billion, compared with the Navy's estimate of $12.5 billion....

The final cost of the CVN-78 could be higher or lower than CBO's estimate. Possible reasons for a higher cost include the following:

— The costs of many lead ships built in the past 20 years have increased more than 30 percent from the original budgeted estimate. CBO's estimate of the cost of the CVN-78 incorporates an amount of growth that falls within the range of historical cost growth for lead ships. However, construction of the ship is only about 60 percent complete, and costs have tended to rise more in the latter stages of ship construction, when systems are being installed and integrated.

— The Navy has stated that there is a 50 percent probability that the cost of the CVN-78 will exceed its estimate. Specifically, in its most recent Selected Acquisition Report, the Navy stated that it has budgeted an amount for the CVN-78 that covers up to the 50th percentile of possible cost outcomes. By comparison, in a written response to CBO and the Congressional Research Service last year, the Navy stated that it had budgeted an amount "greater than [the] 50th percentile" (though without specifying how much greater).

— The Navy has stated that the test program for the carrier could reveal one or more major, possibly expensive, problems.

Possible reasons for a lower cost than CBO's estimate include the following:

— The Navy and the builder of the CVN-78 recognize that cost growth for lead ships is a significant concern, and they are actively managing the CVN-78 program to restrain costs.

— All of the materials for the CVN-78 have been purchased, and much of the equipment for the vessel is being purchased under fixed-price contracts—which essentially eliminates the risk of further cost growth for about half of the projected cost of the carrier.

— A successful test program that revealed only minor problems would likely limit additional costs to less than $100 million.

The next carrier following the CVN-78 will be the CVN-79, the John F. Kennedy. Funding for that ship began in 2007, the Congress officially authorized its construction in 2013, and appropriations for it are expected to be complete by 2018. The Navy estimates that the ship will cost $10.2 billion in 2013 dollars, or $11.3 billion in nominal dollars. In its new Selected Acquisition Report on the CVN-79, the Navy describes its cost estimate as an "aggressive but achievable target." In contrast, CBO estimates that the cost of the ship will be $11.3

billion in 2013 dollars, or about 10 percent more than the Navy's estimate, and $12.0 billion in nominal dollars.[10]

September 2013 GAO Report

A September 2013 GAO report on the CVN-78 program stated the following regarding the potential for further cost growth on CVN-78:

> While construction of CVN 78 is more than halfway complete, the Navy and shipbuilder must still overcome significant technology development, design, and construction challenges in order to deliver a fully functional ship to the fleet at the currently budgeted cost of $12.8 billion and the February 2016 delivery date. However, several critical technologies—provided to the shipbuilder by the Navy—have encountered developmental delays and, subsequently, have not yet reached a level of maturity that will enable them to be effectively incorporated onto the ship. These delays are most evident in the land-based test programs for these technologies, which are lagging significantly behind schedule. At the same time, the ship's design stability—a key factor in controlling future cost growth—is contingent on critical technologies maturing in the configurations currently anticipated. In addition, construction inefficiencies at the shipyard have delayed—and threaten additional delays to—ship launch and delivery. These combined challenges and uncertainties suggest that more cost growth could occur for CVN 78....

> Prior to the CVN 78 detail design contract award, the Navy had only built, tested, and integrated prototype components of the volume search radar in controlled laboratory environments. As we previously reported, these tests revealed deficiencies related to key components of the radar. Under the Navy's 2008 program schedule, the volume search radar was to be developed and tested as part of the Zumwalt-class destroyer program and was expected to approach maturity following land-based testing in fiscal year 2009. The radar would then participate in combat system integration testing with the other major component of the dual band radar, the multifunction radar, and eventually demonstrate maturity as part of Zumwalt-class destroyer at-sea testing in fiscal year 2014. In 2010, however, to reduce Zumwalt-class construction costs, the Navy removed the volume search radar from the destroyer program and suspended remaining land-based testing, leaving key Ford-class testing requirements unaddressed. The Navy subsequently transferred remaining development work to the Ford class program and planned to resume land-based testing in fiscal year 2012 using an actual production unit of the radar—but contracting delays pushed the start of this testing out to fiscal year 2013. As a result of this delay, and the Navy's desire not to slow down the current radar installation schedule for CVN 78, remaining land-based testing will be completed in fiscal year 2014, 4.5 years later than originally planned, using a less capable developmental radar array than the actual production configuration that will be installed on CVN 78. The Navy has also scheduled shipboard testing beginning in fiscal year 2016 to complete additional volume search radar testing not executed on land. This testing schedule increases the risk that discovery of problems with the system will trigger costly design changes and rework aboard the ship....

> Unlike the other critical technologies discussed above, [the EMALS] system was approaching maturity prior to the CVN 78 detail design contract award because the Navy had built and tested competitive prototypes of the system as part of the contractor selection process for EMALS development in 2004. Under the Navy's 2008 program schedule, land-based testing for the system was scheduled to occur between fiscal years 2008 and 2011.

---

[10] Congressional Budget Office, *An Analysis of the Navy's Fiscal Year 2014 Shipbuilding Plan*, October 2013, pp. 20-21.

However, technical issues affecting the EMALS power interface and conversion systems, among other deficiencies, have slowed progress. The Navy's 2012 development schedule calls for land-based testing to continue into fiscal year 2014, which, upon completion, the Navy expects will mature the EMALS technology. In the meantime, however, significant numbers of EMALS components have already been produced, delivered to the shipbuilder, and installed on CVN 78—even though the functional requirements, performance, and suitability of the system remain unproven....

The CVN 78 shipbuilder completed its 3D product model in November 2009—over a year after the construction contract was awarded. At contract award, 76 percent of the model was complete and the shipbuilder had already begun construction of at least 25 percent of its structural units under the previous construction preparation contract. While the model is now considered functionally complete, maintaining design stability depends on the critical technologies discussed above fitting within the space, weight, cooling, and power reservations allotted them. To date, evolving information about the attributes of these technologies has produced a weight/stability configuration for CVN 78 that leaves little margin to incorporate additional weight growth high up in the ship without making corresponding weight trade-offs elsewhere or compromising the future growth potential of the ship. Shipbuilder representatives have recently expressed concern about this possibility, particularly regarding additional design changes to critical technologies still in development—including the volume search radar, advanced arresting gear, and EMALS technologies. According to shipbuilder representatives, additional weight growth to the advanced arresting gear was of particular concern and could trigger a need for future structural and space modifications around the installed system. Further, until the advanced weapons elevators, joint precision approach and landing system, and evolved sea sparrow missile weapons link each demonstrate maturity, the likelihood of additional design changes to CVN 78 persists....

The Navy has taken steps to limit cost growth for EMALS and the advanced arresting gear, which are being developed and produced under contracts separate from the CVN 78 detail design and construction contract. Most notably, in 2010, the Navy negotiated firm fixed-price contracts for production of these systems for CVN 78. According to the Navy, these contracts have helped cap cost growth for these systems and have incentivized more timely deliveries to the shipyard. While EMALS is farther along in development than both the dual band radar and advanced arresting gear systems, all have experienced significant cost growth, and costs are likely to increase, given the remaining work needed to fully develop, test, and integrate the systems on CVN 78. This potential for additional cost growth is also apparent based on the Navy's experience with the most recent Nimitz-class carrier, CVN 77. That ship experienced cost growth during its system integration, even though that effort employed mostly nondevelopmental systems.

Aside from the risk of cost growth stemming from the integration of critical technology systems into the ship, the shipbuilder's cost and schedule performance under the detail design and construction contract suggests additional overruns are looming. Our review of the contractor's earned value management data for the program indicates that shipbuilder cost pressures remain high and additional costs are likely, especially as key developmental items are integrated onto the ship. We reviewed 18 months of earned value management data for the CVN 78 ship program during the period of July 2011 through December 2012. During this time, the shipbuilder increased its estimate of the number of labor hours required to construct CVN 78 from 44.4 million to 47.3 million. Consequently, the shipbuilder's budgeted cost grew substantially, from $4,758 million to $5,266 million (an increase of $508 million). Our analysis shows that, as of December 2012, the contractor was forecasting an overrun at contract completion of over $913 million. This cost growth is attributable to the shipbuilder not accomplishing work as planned. The Navy has largely, but not fully, funded this cost growth within CVN 78's $12.8 billion procurement budget.

Further, the Navy's current budget estimate of $12.8 billion for completing CVN 78 is optimistic because it assumes the shipbuilder will maintain its current level of performance throughout the remainder of construction. This assumption is inconsistent with historical Navy shipbuilding experiences for recent lead ships, which have suffered from performance degradation late in construction. Our previous work has shown that the full extent of cost growth does not usually manifest itself until after the ship is more than 60 percent complete, when key systems are being installed and integrated. In April 2013, the ship was 56 percent complete. The Director of DOD's Cost Assessment and Program Evaluation office and the Congressional Budget Office—as well as Navy cost analysts and a Navy-commissioned expert panel—have also projected higher than budgeted procurement costs for CVN 78, with cost estimates ranging from $13.0 to $14.2 billion.[11]

The report stated the following regarding the potential for further cost growth on CVN-79:

> The Navy and shipbuilder are implementing changes to the build strategy for CVN 79 aimed at reducing that ship's costs before the construction contract is awarded, currently planned for September 2013. These changes include increased time allotted to construct the ship and in-yard construction process improvements. Remaining technical and design risks with CVN 78, however, could interfere with the Navy's ability to achieve its desired cost savings for CVN 79. These uncertainties also affect the Navy and contractor's ability to assess the likely CVN 79 costs ahead of contract award and, when coupled with the existing sole source environment for aircraft carrier construction, compromise the government's negotiating position for CVN 79.
>
> The Navy and its shipbuilder have learned valuable lessons from CVN 78 construction that have the potential to improve cost outcomes for the construction of the first follow-on ship, CVN 79. The shipbuilder plans to employ a new build strategy for CVN 79 that (1) allots more time to fund and construct the ship compared to CVN 78 and (2) implements process improvements aimed at completing more work earlier in the build process—steps that the Navy anticipates will achieve construction efficiency improvements as compared to CVN 78. However, remaining technical and design risks in the program could undermine the Navy's ability to realize cost savings on CVN 79....
>
> The Navy's decision to fund CVN 79 construction over 6 years was coupled with a decision to increase the build time for the ship as compared to CVN 78. According to the Navy, it will use the additional time to improve CVN 79's construction sequence and implement cost reduction initiatives. Further, Ford class shipbuilders report that the increased time afforded to CVN 79 construction provides additional opportunities to apply lessons learned from lead ship construction. The Navy expects the combined savings from these actions to more than offset the increased costs associated with extending the funding of the ship by 2 years. Figure 9 compares CVN 78 and CVN 79 construction schedules....
>
> As part of CVN 79 construction, the shipbuilder plans to implement process improvements aimed at reducing the labor hours—and cost—required to construct the ship, as compared to CVN 78....
>
> The core of the shipbuilder's strategy for CVN 79 is moving more planned work—including complex ship assemblies—earlier in the build process so that it can be completed in shipyard workshops. Generally, the earlier work can be sequenced in the build process, the more efficiently it can be completed....

---

[11] Government Accountability Office, *Ford-Class Carriers[:] Lead Ship Testing and Reliability Shortfalls Will Limit Initial Fleet Capabilities*, GAO-13-396, September 2013, pp. 11, 16-17, 18, 20-21, 27-28.

Although the Navy and shipbuilder expect CVN 79's design to be virtually the same as that of the lead ship—another step toward improving follow-on ship outcomes—remaining developmental and design risks in the program could undermine the actual realization of cost savings. As discussed above, these risks are exemplified by key ship systems not progressing through their land-based test programs at the pace the Navy anticipated—delays largely attributable to persisting technical deficiencies. Navy and shipbuilder efforts to resolve these deficiencies on CVN 78—concurrent with follow-on ship construction—are likely to lead to redesign and potentially costly out of sequence work or rework for CVN 79. If these discoveries and fixes disrupt CVN 79 construction and offset planned improvements, they could jeopardize the Navy's ability to complete the ship within planned cost and schedule estimates.

The Navy's cost estimate for CVN 79 detail design and construction is closely linked to CVN 78 outcomes and reflects an expectation that the shipbuilder will deliver the lead ship within current labor hour estimates. One key component of the CVN 79 cost estimate is a Navy assumption that 15 percent fewer labor hours will be required to construct the follow-on ship as compared to the lead ship. This estimate is also underpinned by expectations that the shipbuilder's current level of performance will persist between now and lead ship delivery. Further, the Navy's budget for CVN 79 is predicated on even higher performance gains than those forecast in the cost estimate—notably, 20 percent fewer labor hours in construction as compared to CVN 78. Yet, as we previously detailed, the Navy's understanding of the costs required to construct and deliver CVN 78 remains incomplete. These knowledge gaps add risk and uncertainty to CVN 79 cost and budget estimates.[12]

June 2013 Press Report

A June 27, 2013, press report stated:

> The U.S. Navy should delay the award of a multibillion-dollar contract to Huntington Ingalls Industries Inc.to build the second aircraft carrier in a new class as the first one faces failings from its radar to the gear that launches planes, congressional investigators said.
>
> "Technical, design and construction challenges" with the first carrier, the USS Gerald R. Ford, have caused "significant cost increases and reduce the likelihood that a fully functional ship will be delivered on time," the Government Accountability Office said in a draft report obtained by Bloomberg News....
>
> Delays and "reliability deficiencies" with the flattop's new dual-mission radar, electromagnetic launch system and arresting gear for aircraft mean that the Ford "will likely face operational limitations that extend past commissioning" in March 2016 and "into initial deployments," the agency said.
>
> The GAO, the investigative arm of Congress, said that's reason enough to delay the contract that's scheduled to be issued this year for the second ship, the USS John F. Kennedy....
>
> "It will be important to avoid repeating mistakes" in the contract for the Kennedy, the GAO said. "Staying within budget" will require the Navy to reduce "significant risk mainly by completing land-based testing for critical technologies before negotiating a contract" with Newport News, Virginia-based Huntington Ingalls.

---

[12] Government Accountability Office, *Ford-Class Carriers[:] Lead Ship Testing and Reliability Shortfalls Will Limit Initial Fleet Capabilities*, GAO-13-396, September 2013, pp. 41-42, 43, 44-45.

Beci Brenton, a company spokeswoman, said in a telephone interview that "it would not be appropriate to comment on a draft report." Naval Sea Systems Command spokeswoman Colleen O'Rourke[13] said in a statement that "as the Navy is currently working with the GAO on this report, it would be inappropriate to comment on any draft findings at this time. When the report is finalized, it will include Navy comments."

The Navy remains committed to the Ford-class carrier as a needed capability, said a Navy official who declined to be identified before the GAO releases its final report. The Navy is confident that the first vessel will be delivered on schedule and that lessons learned from building it will be applied to reduce the cost of the second ship, the official said....

While the GAO said that the Navy and Huntington Ingalls are taking steps to control costs for the Ford, most increases occur after a vessel is 60 percent complete and key systems are installed and integrated. The Ford is now 56 percent complete.

Even the current $12.8 billion estimate is "optimistic because it assumes the shipbuilder will maintain its current level of performance throughout the remainder of construction," the GAO said....

The Pentagon's independent cost-estimating office, the Congressional Budget Office and a Navy-commissioned panel project final costs as high as $14.2 billion, the GAO said....

"As it now stands, the Navy will not be positioned to deliver a fully capable ship at the time," the GAO said.

"Reliability shortfalls facing key Ford-class systems cloud the Navy's ability to forecast when, or if" the carrier will meet the aircraft sortie rates and reduced manning requirements that distinguish it from the older Nimitz class, the GAO said. O'Rourke, the Naval Sea Systems Command spokeswoman, wouldn't comment on the specific value of the potential detailed design and construction contract to Huntington Ingalls for the Kennedy that the GAO said is due in September....

The largest share of the cost increase for the Ford, 38 percent, stemmed from technologies delivered by the Navy, including the radar, launch system and arresting gear, according to the GAO.

The electromagnetic launch system made by San Diego-based General Atomics has increased to $742.6 million, up 134 percent since 2008, the GAO said. The cost of arresting gear also made by the company increased 125 percent to $169 million.

Raytheon Co.'s dual-band radar has increased 140 percent to $484 million, according to data cited by the GAO. Twenty-seven percent of the cost growth was pegged to shipbuilder design issues and another 27 percent to construction, both attributed to Huntington Ingalls.

Huntington Ingalls is building the Ford under a $4.9 billion detailed design contract that covers the shipbuilder's portion of constructing the vessel. It doesn't cover other costs, such as the nuclear reactor to power the ship and other government-furnished equipment....

The GAO said its analysis indicates that Huntington Ingalls "was forecasting an overrun at contract completion of over $913 million" that it said stemmed from "the shipbuilder not accomplishing work as planned."

---

[13] Colleen O'Rourke is not related to Ronald O'Rourke.

Huntington's Brenton said in an e-mail in May that, "as the first new design carrier beginning construction in more than 40 years," the Ford "is designed to provide increased capability and reduced total ownership cost by about $4 billion compared to Nimitz-class carriers."

"For this first-of-class ship, construction commenced in parallel with design completion based on earlier decisions at Department of Defense," she said. "Ongoing design during the construction process caused delay and inefficiencies in procurement, manufacturing, and assembly."[14]

March 2013 Navy Report to Congress (Released May 2013)

A March 2013 report to Congress on the Navy's plan for building CVN-79 that was released to the public on May 16, 2013, states in its executive summary:

> As a result of the lessons learned on CVN 78, the approach to carrier construction has undergone an extensive affordability review and the Navy and the shipbuilder have made significant changes on CVN 79 that will significantly reduce the cost to build the ship. These include four key construction areas:
>
> — CVN 79 construction will start with a complete design and a complete bill of material
>
> — CVN 79 construction will start with a firm set of stable requirements
>
> — CVN 79 construction will start with the development complete on a host of new technologies inserted on CVN 78 ranging from the Electromagnetic Aircraft Launch System (EMALS), the Dual Band Radar, and the reactor plant, to key valves in systems throughout the ship
>
> — CVN 79 construction will start with an 'optimal build' plan that emphasizes the completion of work and ship outfitting as early as possible in the construction process to optimize cost and ultimately schedule performance.
>
> In addition to these fundamentals, the Navy and the shipbuilder are tackling cost through a series of other changes that when taken over the entire carrier will have a significant impact on construction costs. The Navy has also imposed cost targets and is aggressively pursuing cost reduction initiatives in its government furnished systems. A detailed accounting of these actions is included in this report.
>
> The actions discussed in this report are expected to reduce the material cost of CVN 79 by 10-20% in real terms from CVN 78, to reduce the number of man-hours required to build the CVN 79 by 15-25% from CVN 78, and to reduce the cost of government furnished systems by 5-10% in real terms from CVN 78.[15]

For the full text of the navy's report, see **Appendix A**.

---

[14] Tony Capaccio, "Navy Should Delay Next Carrier Amid Troubles, GAO Says," *Bloomberg.com*, June 27, 2013.

[15] *Aircraft Carrier Construction, John F Kennedy (CVN 79), Report to Congress*, March 2013, p. 3. An annotation on the report's cover page indicates that the report was authorized for public release on May 16, 2013. The report was posted at InsideDefense.com (subscription required) on June 21, 2013. See also Megan Eckstein, "Navy Plan To Congress Outlines New Strategies To Save On CVN-79," *Inside the Navy*, June 24, 2013.

December 31, 2012, DOD SAR (Released May 2013)

The December 31, 2012, DOD Selected Acquisition Report (SAR) for the CVN-78 program, which was released in May 2013, states:

> The CVN 78 is experiencing cost growth due to "first of class" material availability (i.e., valves, actuators), construction labor inefficiencies, and challenges associated with concurrent development and integration of new Government Furnished Equipment (GFE) and Contractor Furnished Equipment (CFE) systems during lead ship design and construction. For material costs, the variance reflects challenges associated with a shrinking supplier base, procurement of developmental contractor furnished components, and vendor qualification on CVN 78 unique items. Labor inefficiencies are the result of "first of class" challenges. The effect of new and thinner steels on structural erection was greater than expected, slowing production and requiring more hours than planned for straightening, temporary structure and rigging. HII-NNS also experienced "first of class" learning associated with the new CVN 78 Class modular build strategy, including movement, blast and coat, and assembly area footprint difficulties for larger, reconfigured CVN 78 structural units. Delays in the delivery of new developmental components as well as engineering products required to develop construction work package also inhibited labor performance.

> During 2012, HII-NNS continued its design and production efforts on CVN 78. Quarterly Progress Reviews were held to manage and assess the status of design and production on CVN 78. As of February 17, 2013, the construction effort was 67.3% complete based on contract dollars. The landing of the island occurred on January 26, 2013. The shipbuilder has proposed a revised Estimate at Completion (EAC) increasing Direct Labor from 43.9 to 47.3 million man hours that incorporates their assessment of performance trends and associated recovery efforts for both construction and support areas. The Navy is evaluating this proposed increase with emphasis on mitigating key cost and schedule drivers. The Navy continues to work with the Participating Acquisition Resource Managers (PARMs) to identify and remove barriers to improve cost and schedule performance for the new developmental GFE systems. HII-NNS has rescheduled the CVN 78 launch from July 2013 to November 2013. Although shipbuilder actions to resolve "first of class" issues have retired some technical and schedule risk, HII-NNS has been unable to retire all schedule risk, resulting in a four month delay to the launch of CVN 78, with associated impact to delivery. The Navy agrees with the delay to launch. Delivery is expected to be delayed until approximately 2nd Quarter FY 2016.

> The Navy is submitting reports to the four defense committees addressing cost performance of the CVN 78 detail design and construction in response to Senator John McCain's letter of August 11, 2011. At the direction of the Assistant Secretary of the Navy for Research, Development and Acquisition (ASN(RD&A)), an independent team conducted an end-to-end assessment of CVN 78 cost variance that included opportunities to prevent further increases. Recommendations from the report, briefed to ASN(RD&A) on December 21, 2011, are being implemented. Recommendations from the CVN 78 end to end reviews have been consolidated into 38 actionable items that are been tracked to completion. As of March 18, 2013, 17 recommendations have been implemented with 21 recommendations in progress. All recommendations are expected to be implemented by September 2014. The review team reconvened in 2012 and concluded the program offices action plan adequately addresses their recommendations.

> The high level of design maturity and material certification for the CVN 79 provides a stable technical baseline for material procurement cost and schedule performance, which supports the development and execution of an improved and reliable build plan. The Construction Preparation (CP) Contract for CVN 79 advance procurement research, design, and

engineering was awarded on January 15, 2009. An extension to CP efforts through FY 2013 was awarded in March 2013.

To enable full ship-set material buys for cost reduction benefits and to ensure material availability, two material procurement contract modifications were awarded to HII-NNS during FY 2012. A third material procurement award was executed in March 2013. CVN 79 affordability is being driven through several areas. The CVN 79 is a design roll-over from CVN 78, with changes for improved producibility, reduced cost, and limited fact-of-life obsolescence issues. Lessons learned during the construction of CVN 78 are resulting in changes to the CVN 79 build plan to improve production efficiency. In addition, production improvements are being achieved through implementation of several initiatives aimed at driving work to be executed at the most efficient time (typically in the shop or on the platen rather than in the dry-dock or after launch), as well as driving learning curve performance into subsets of the ship construction (creation of "families of units" and work cells). In the aggregate, the plan for CVN 79 construction will substantially drive down costs.

The CVN 79 DD&C Request for Proposal (RFP) was provided to HII-NNS on October 2, 2012. The CVN 79 DD&C contract is planned for award in September 2013. Unlike the CVN 78 DD&C which is a Cost Plus Incentive Fee (CPIF) contract, the Navy plans to negotiate a Fixed Price Incentive (FPI) contract with a simplified structure for CVN 79.[16]

The SAR also states:

The CVN 79 is budgeted at an aggressive but achievable target.

The Navy and shipbuilder have made fundamental change in the manner in which the CVN 79 will be built to incorporate lessons learned from CVN 78 and eliminate the key contributors to cost performance challenges realized in the construction of CVN 78. The approach to carrier construction has undergone an extensive affordability review, the results of which are reflected in the CVN 79 budget. Further improvements are planned for CVN 80 but have not yet been incorporated into the CVN 80 cost estimates. The Navy is committed to driving down aircraft carrier construction costs, and fully expects future estimates for CVN 80 to reflect a continued downward trend.[17]

Regarding a contract that NNS has with the Navy for detailed design and construction (DD&C) work on CVN-78—a contract that accounts for a portion of the ship's total cost—the SAR states that the value of the contract has grown from an initial price of $4,910.5 million to a current price of $5,885.6 million, and that NNS and the Navy estimate that the price will grow further, to $6,665.6 million (NNS's estimate) or $6,638.7 million (the Navy's estimate) by the time the contract is completed (i.e., estimated price at completion).[18] In discussing these figures, the SAR states:

The unfavorable net change in the cost variance is due to material cost growth (86%), labor inefficiencies (25%), Overhead improvement (-3%), and Facilities Capital Cost of Money (FCCM) improvement (-8%). The material variances are due to market forces, unanticipated impacts of a "first of class" specification on contractor furnished material costs (e.g. valves, electrical components, steel and other commodities), and refined understanding of material requirements as the ship design matured. Labor inefficiencies are the result of "first of class"

---

[16] Department of Defense, *Selected Acquisition Report (SAR), CVN 78 Class*, December 31, 2012, pp. 5-6.

[17] Department of Defense, *Selected Acquisition Report (SAR), CVN 78 Class*, December 31, 2012, p. 30.

[18] Department of Defense, *Selected Acquisition Report (SAR), CVN 78 Class*, December 31, 2012, p. 56.

challenges including producibility issues (e.g. thin plate steel, weld distortion, and the increased use of temporary structures and rigging). Additionally, increased supervision has been required to manage the above challenges and a developing workforce.

The favorable net change in the schedule variance is due to improvement in material availability and the overall decrease in design hold ups, which have resulted in a significant increase in workable work packages available to the assembly trades. This increase in available work, coupled with the significant increase in manning and improved performance of the assembly trades, has resulted in an overall improvement in schedule performance.[19]

May 2013 Navy Testimony

In its prepared statement for a May 8, 2013, hearing on Navy shipbuilding programs before the Seapower subcommittee of the Senate Armed Services Committee, the Navy stated that

> In 2011, the Navy identified spiraling cost growth [on CVN-78] associated with first of class non-recurring design, contractor and government furnished equipment, and ship production issues on the lead ship. The Navy completed an end-to-end review of CVN 78 construction in December 2011 and, with the shipbuilder, implemented a series of corrective actions to stem, and to the extent possible, reverse these trends. While cost performance has stabilized, incurred cost growth is irreversible....
>
> As a result of lessons learned on CVN 78, the approach to carrier construction has undergone an extensive affordability review; and the Navy and the shipbuilder have made significant changes on CVN 79 that will reduce the cost to build the ship. CVN 79 construction will start with a complete design, firm requirements, and material economically procured and on hand in support of production need. The ship's build schedule also provides for increased completion levels at each stage of construction with resulting improved production efficiencies....
>
> Inarguably, this new class of aircraft carrier brings forward tremendous capability and life-cycle cost advantages compared to the NIMITZ-class it will replace. However, the design, development and construction efforts required to overcome the technical challenges inherent to these advanced capabilities have significantly impacted cost performance on the lead ship. The Navy continues implementing actions from the 2012 detailed review of the FORD-Class build plan to control cost and improve performance across lead and follow ship contracts. This effort, taken in conjunction with a series of corrective actions with the shipbuilder on the lead ship, will not recover costs to original targets for GERALD R. FORD [CVN-78], but should improve performance on the lead ship while fully benefitting CVN 79 and following ships of the class.[20]

In the discussion portion of the hearing, Sean Stackley, the Assistant Secretary of the Navy for Research, Development and Acquisition (i.e., the Navy's acquisition executive), testified that

---

[19] Department of Defense, *Selected Acquisition Report (SAR), CVN 78 Class*, December 31, 2012, p. 56.

[20] Statement of The Honorable Sean J. Stackley, Assistant Secretary of the Navy (Research, Development and Acquisition) and Vice Admiral Allen G. Myers, Deputy Chief of Naval Operations for Integration of Capabilities and Resources and Vice Admiral Kevin M. McCoy, Commander, Naval Sea Systems Command, Before the Subcommittee on Seapower of the Senate Armed Services Committee on Department of the Navy Shipbuilding Programs, May 8, 2013, p. 8.

First, the cost growth on the CVN-78 is unacceptable. The cost growth dates back in time to the very basic concepts that went into take in the Nimitz-class and doing a total redesign of the Nimitz class to get to a level of capability and to reduce operating and support cost for the future carrier. Far too much risk was carried into the design of the first of the Ford-class.

Cost growth stems to the design was moving at the time production started. The vendor base that was responsible for delivering new components and material to support the ship production was (inaudible) with new developments in the vendor base and production plan do not account for the material ordering difficulties, the material delivery difficulties and some of the challenges associated with building a whole new design compared to the Nimitz....

Sir, for CVN-79, we have—we have held up the expenditures on CVN-79 as we go through the details of—one, ensuring that the design of the 78 is complete and repeated for the 79s [sic] that we start with a clean design.

Two, we're going through the material procurement. We brought a third party into assessment material-buying practices at Newport News to bring down the cost of material. And we're metering out the dollars for buying material until it hits the objectives that we're setting for CVN-79 through rewriting the build plan on CVN-79.

If you take a look at how the 78 is being constructed, far too much work is being accomplished late in the build cycle. So we are rewriting the build plan for CVN-79, do more work in the shops where it's more efficient, more work in the buildings where it's more efficient, less work in the dry dock, less work on the water. And then we're going after the rates—the labor rates and the investments needed by the shipbuilder to achieve these efficiencies.[21]

Later in the hearing, Stackley testified that

the history in shipbuilding is since you don't have a prototype for a new ship, the first of class referred to as the lead ship is your prototype. And so you carry a lot of risk into the construction of that first of class.

Also, given the nature that there's a lengthy design development and build span associated with ships, so there is a certain amount of overlap or concurrency that occurs between the development of new systems that need to be delivered with the first ship, the incorporation of the design of those new systems and the actual construction. And so to the extent that there is change in a new ship class then the risk goes up accordingly.

In the case of the CVN-78, the degree of change compared to the Nimitz was fairly extraordinary all for good reasons, good intentions, increased capability, increased survivability, significant reduction in operating and support costs. So there was a determination that will take on this risk in order to get those benefits, and the case of the CVN-78, those risks are driving a lot of the cost growth on the lead ship.

When you think about the follow ships, now you've got a stable design, now your vendor base has got a production line going to support the production. Now you've got a build plan and a workforce that has climbed up on the learning curve to drive cost down. So you can look at—you can look at virtually every shipbuilding program and you'll see a significant drop-off in cost from that first of class to the follow ships.

---

[21] Transcript of hearing.

And then you look for a stable learning curve to take over in the longer term production of a ship class.

Carriers are unique for a number of reasons, one of which we don't have an annual procurement of carriers. They're spread out over a five and, in fact, in the case of 78 as much as seven-year period. So in order to achieve that learning, there are additional challenges associated with achieving that learning. And so we're going at it very deliberately on the CVN-79 through the build plan with the shipbuilder to hit the line that we've got to have— the cost reductions that we've got to have on the follow ships of the class.[22]

November 2012 Press Report

A November 29, 2012, press report stated:

Huntington Ingalls Industries Inc. will miss its 2012 target for reducing costs on the USS Gerald R. Ford, the aircraft carrier that will be the most expensive U.S. warship.

The shipbuilder will fall short of getting 86 cents of planned work accomplished for every dollar spent, in part because of late component deliveries from subcontractors, according to the Navy admiral responsible for carrier development and construction....

"They have continued to improve in the right direction, but they did not make it to 86" percent, Rear Admiral Thomas Moore, the Navy's program executive officer for aircraft carriers, said in a phone interview. The Navy hopes the company will eventually get $1 of value from every $1 spent, he said....

"There are many challenges" in building a prototype that's also the first production vessel of a three-ship class, Beci Brenton, a spokeswoman for the Newport News, Virginia-based company, said in an e-mailed statement.

The company "has developed and implemented a host of improvement actions" this year, she said. "We have continued to advance the shipbuilding industry in tooling, material controls and craft performance through the use of innovation in technology, process changes and teaming."...

Huntington Ingalls' cost efficiency goals have been "challenging but attainable, and they met them and did well in 2011," Moore said. "They did not meet all those goals in 2012, and we will sit down and figure out where we are going with them in 2013."

Reaching the 86 percent mark would have helped reduce what's now an estimated $884 million overrun on the design and construction contract. The Navy's share is $690 million. Huntington's share is $194 million, which would be forfeited if the overrun isn't reduced.

Moore said Huntington Ingalls' failure to hit its efficiency goal this year won't increase the cost estimate for the next carrier in the class, the USS John F. Kennedy.

"My expectation is that we are starting with a clean sheet of paper," he said. "I fully expect" the second carrier's costs "to be significantly below where we end up on," the Ford, he said.[23]

---

[22] Transcript of hearing.

[23] Tony Capaccio, "Huntington Ingalls Aircraft Carrier To Miss Cost-Reduction Goal," *Bloomberg Government* (continued...)

March 2012 Navy Letter to Senator McCain

Secretary of the Navy Ray Mabus, in a letter with attachment sent in late March 2012 to Senator John McCain on controlling cost growth in CVN-78, stated:

> Dear Senator McCain:
>
> Thank you for your letter of March 21, 2012, regarding the first-of-class aircraft carrier, GERALD R. FORD (CVN 78). Few major programs carry greater importance or greater impact on national security, and no other major program comprises greater scale and complexity than the Navy's nuclear aircraft carrier program. Accordingly, successful execution of this program carries the highest priority within the Department of the Navy.
>
> I have shared in the past my concern when I took office and learned the full magnitude of new technologies and design change being brought to the FORD. Requirements drawn up more than a decade prior for this capital ship drove development of a new reactor plant, propulsion system, electric plant and power distribution system, first of kind electromagnetic aircraft launching system, advanced arresting gear, integrated warfare system including a new radar and communications suite, air conditioning plant, weapons elevators, topside design, survivability improvements, and all new interior arrangements. CVN 78 is a near-total redesign of the NIMITZ Class she replaces. Further, these major developments, which were to be incrementally introduced in the program, were directed in 2002 to be integrated into CVN 78 in a single step. Today we are confronting the cost impacts of these decisions made more than a decade ago.
>
> In my August 29, 2011 letter, I provided details regarding these cost impacts. At that time, I reported the current estimate for the Navy's share of the shipbuilder's construction overrun, $690 million, and described that I had directed an end-to-end review to identify the changes necessary to improve cost for carrier design, material procurement, planning, build and test. The attached white paper provides the findings of that review and the steps we are taking to drive affordability into the remaining CVN 78 construction effort. Pending the results of these efforts, the Navy has included the 'fact of life' portion of the stated overrun in the Fiscal Year 2013 President's Budget request. The review also highlighted the compounding effects of applying traditional carrier build planning to a radically new design; the challenges inherent to low-rate, sole-source carrier procurement; and the impact of external economic factors accrued over 15 years of CVN 78 procurement—all within the framework of cost-plus contracts. The outlined approach for ensuring CVN 79 and follow ship affordability focuses equally upon tackling these issues while applying the many lessons learned in the course of CVN 78 procurement.
>
> As always, if I may be of further assistance, please let me know.
>
> Sincerely, [signed] Ray Mabus
>
> Attachment: As stated
>
> Copy to: The Honorable Carl Levin, Chairman
>
> [Attachment]

(...continued)

(bgov.com), November 29, 2012.

Improving Cost Performance on CVN 78

CVN 78 is nearing 40 percent completion. Cost growth to-date is attributable to increases in design, contractor furnished material, government furnished material (notably, the Electromagnetic Aircraft Launching System (EMALS), Advanced Arresting Gear (AAG), and the Dual Band Radar (DBR)), and production labor performance. To achieve the best case outcome, the program must execute with zero additional cost growth in design and material procurement, and must improve production performance. The Navy and the shipbuilder have implemented a series of actions and initiatives in the management and oversight of CVN 78 that cross the full span of contracting, design, material procurement, government furnished equipment, production planning, production, management and oversight.

CVN 78 is being procured within a framework of cost-plus contracts. Within this framework, however, the recent series of action taken by the Navy to improve contract effectiveness are achieving the desired effect of incentivizing improved cost performance and reducing government exposure to further cost growth.

- CVN 78 design has been converted from a 'level of effort, fixed fee' contract to a completion contract with a firm target and incentive fee. Shipbuilder cost performance has been on-target or better since this contract was changed.

- CVN 78 construction fee has been retracted, consistent with contract performance. However, the shipbuilder is incentivized by the contract shareline to improve upon current performance to meet agreed-to cost goals.

- Contract design changes are under strict control; authorized only for safety, damage control, mission-degrading deficiencies, or similar. Adjudicated changes have been contained to less than 1 percent of contract target price.

- The Navy converted the EMALS and AAG production contract to a firm, fixed price contract, capping cost growth to that system and imposing negative incentives for late delivery.

- Naval Sea Systems Command is performing a review of carrier specifications with the shipbuilder, removing or improving upon overly burdensome or unneeded specifications that impose unnecessary cost on the program.

The single largest impact to cost performance to-date has been contractor and government material cost overruns. These issues trace to lead ship complexity and CVN 78 concurrency, but they also point to inadequate accountability for carrier material procurement, primarily during the ship's advance procurement period (2002-2008).

These effects cannot be reversed on CVN 78, but it is essential to improve upon material delivery to the shipyard to mitigate the significant impact of material delays on production performance. Equally important, the systemic material procurement deficiencies must be corrected for CVN 79. To this end, the Navy and shipbuilder have taken the following actions.

- The Navy has employed outside supply chain management experts to develop optimal material procurement strategies. The Navy and the shipbuilder are reviewing remaining material requirements to employ these best practices (structuring procurements to achieve quantity discounts, dual-sourcing to improve schedule performance and leverage competitive opportunities, etc.).

- The shipbuilder has assigned engineering and material sourcing personnel to each of their key vendors to expedite component qualifications and delivery to the shipyard.

- The shipbuilder is inventorying all excess material procured on CVN 78 for transfer to CVN 79 (cost reduction to CVN 78), as applicable.

- The Program Executive Officer (Carriers) is conducting quarterly flag-level government furnished equipment summits to drive cost reduction opportunities and ensure on-time delivery of required equipment and design information to the shipbuilder.

The most important finding regarding CVN 78 remaining cost is that the CVN 78 build plan, consistent with the NIMITZ class, focuses foremost on completion of structural and critical path work to support launching the ship on-schedule. This emphasis on structure comes at the expense of completing ship systems, outfitting, and furnishing early in the build process and results in costly, labor-intensive system completion activity during later; more costly stages of production. Achieving the program's cost improvement targets will require that CVN 78 increase its level of completion at launch, from current estimate of 60 percent to no less than 65 percent. To achieve this goal and drive greater focus on system completion:

- the Navy fostered a collaborative build process review by the shipbuilder with other Tier 1 private shipyards in order to benchmark its performance arid identify fundamental changes that would yield marked improvement;

- the shipbuilder has established specific launch metrics by system (foundations, machinery, piping, power panels, vent duct, lighting, etc.) and increased staffing for waterfront engineering and material expediters to support meeting these metrics;

- the shipbuilder has linked all of these processes within a detailed integrated master schedule, providing greater visibility to current performance and greater ability to control future cost and schedule performance across the shipbuilding disciplines;

- the Navy and shipbuilder are conducting Unit Readiness Reviews of CVN 78 erection units to ensure that the outfitted condition of each hull unit being lifted into the dry-dock contains the proper level of outfitting.

These initiatives, which summarize a more detailed list of actions being implemented and tracked as result of the end-to-end review, are accompanied by important management changes.

- The shipbuilder has assigned a new Vice President in charge of CVN 78, a new Vice President in charge of material management and purchasing, and a number of new general shop foreman to strengthen CVN 78 performance.

- The Navy has assigned a second tour Flag Officer with considerable carrier operations, construction, and program management experience as the new Program-Executive Officer (PEO).

- The PEO and shipyard president conduct bi-weekly launch readiness reviews focusing on cost performance, critical path issues and accomplishment of the target for launch completion.

- The Assistant Secretary of the Navy (Research, Development, and Acquisition) conducts a monthly review of program progress and performance with the PEO and shipbuilder, bringing to bear the full weight of the Department, as needed, to ensure that all that can be done to improve on cost performance is being done.

Early production performance improvements can be traced directly to these actions, however, significant further improvement is required. To this end, the Navy is conducting a line-by-line review of all 'cost to-go' on CVN 78 to identify further opportunity to reduce cost and to mitigate risk.

Improving Cost Performance on CVN 79

CVN 79 Advance Procurement commenced in 2007 with early construction activities following in 2011. Authorization for CVN 79 procurement is requested in Fiscal Year 2013 President's Budget request with the first year of incremental funding. Two years have been added to the CVN 79 production schedule in this budget request, afforded by the fact that CVN 79 will replace CVN 68 when she inactivates. To improve affordability for CVN 79, the Navy plans to leverage this added time by introducing a fundamental change to the carrier procurement approach and a corresponding shift to the carrier build plan, while incorporating CVN 78 lessons learned.

The two principal 'documents' which the Navy and shipbuilder must ensure are correct and complete at the outset of CVN 79 procurement are the design and the build plan.

Design is governed by rules in place that no changes will be considered for the follow ship except changes necessary to correct design deficiencies on the lead ship, fact of life changes to correct obsolescence issues, or changes that will result in reduced cost for the follow ship. Exceptions to these rules must be approved by the JROC, or designee. Accordingly, the Navy is requesting procurement authority for CVN 79 with the Design Product Model complete and construction drawings approximately 95 percent complete (compared to approximately 30 percent complete at time of lead ship authorization).

As well, first article testing and certification will be complete for virtually all major new equipments introduced in the FORD Class. At this point in time, the shipbuilder has developed a complete bill of material for CVN 79. The Navy is working with the shipbuilder to ensure that the contractor's material estimates are in-line with Navy 'should cost' estimates; eliminating non-recurring costs embedded in lead ship material, validating quantities, validating escalation indices, incorporating lead ship lessons learned. The Navy has increased its oversight of contractor furnished material procurement, ensuring that material procurement is competed (where competition is available); that it is fixed priced; that commodities are bundled to leverage economic order quantity opportunities; and that the vendor base capacity and schedule for receipt supports the optimal build plan being developed for production.

In total, the high level of design maturity and material certification provides a stable technical baseline for material procurement cost and schedule performance, which are critical to developing and executing an improved, reliable build plan.

In order to significantly improve production labor performance, based on timely receipt of design and material, the Navy and shipbuilder are reviewing and implementing changes to the CVN 79 build plan and affected facilities. The guiding principles are:

- maximize planned work in the shops and early stages of construction;

- revise sequence of structural unit construction to maximize learning curve performance through 'families of units' and work cells;

- incorporate design changes to improve FORD Class producibility;

- increase the size of erection units to eliminate disruptive unit breaks and improve unit alignment and fairness;

- increase outfitting levels for assembled units prior to erection in the dry-dock;

- increase overall ship completion levels at each key event.

The shipbuilder is working on detailed plans for facility improvements that will improve productivity, and the Navy will consider incentives for capital improvements that would provide targeted return on investment, such as:

- increasing the amount of temporary and permanent covered work areas;

- adding ramps and service towers for improved access to work sites and the dry-dock;

- increasing lift capacity to enable construction of larger, more fully outfitted super-lifts:

An incremental improvement to carrier construction cost will fall short of the improvement necessary to ensure affordability for CVN 79 and follow ships. Accordingly, the shipbuilder has established aggressive targets for CVN 79 to drive the game-changing improvements needed for carrier construction. These targets include:

- 75 percent Complete at Launch (15 percent> [i.e., 15 percent greater than] FORD);

- 85-90 percent of cable pulled prior to Launch (25-30 percent> FORD);

- 30 percent increase in front-end shop work (piping details, foundations, etc);

- All structural unit hot work complete prior to blast and paint;

- 25 percent increase to work package throughput;

- 100 percent of material available for all work packages in accordance with the integrated master schedule;

- zero delinquent engineering and planning products;

- resolution of engineering problems in < 8 [i.e., less than 8] hours.

In parallel with efforts to improve shipbuilder costs, the PEO is establishing equally aggressive targets to reduce the cost of government furnished equipment for CVN 79; working equipment item by equipment item with an objective to reduce overall GFE costs by ~$500 million. Likewise, the Naval Sea Systems Command is committed to continuing its ongoing effort to identify specification changes that could significantly reduce cost without compromising safety and technical rigor.

The output of these efforts comprises the optimal build plan for CVN 79 and follow, and will be incorporated in the detail design and construction baseline for CVN 79. CVN 79 will be procured using a fixed price incentive contract.[24]

Issues Raised in January 2014 DOT&E Report

Another issue for Congress concerns CVN-78 program issues that were raised in a January 2014 report from DOD's Director, Operational Test and Evaluation (DOT&E)—DOT&E's annual report for FY2013. The report stated the following in its section on the CVN-78 program:

Assessment

Test Planning

• The current state of the VCVN [Virtual CVN] model does not fully provide for an accurate accounting of SGR [Sortie Generation Rate] due to a lack of fidelity regarding manning and equipment/aircraft availability. Spiral development of the VCVN model continues in order to ensure that the required fidelity will be available to support the SGR assessment during IOT&E [Initial Operational Test and Evaluation].

• A new TEMP [Test and Evaluation Master Plan] is under development to address problems with the currently-approved TEMP. The current TEMP does not adequately address platform-level developmental testing. The Program Office has begun to refine the Post Delivery Test and Trials schedule, but that schedule still lacks sufficient details to ensure reasonable developmental testing. Lack of platform-level developmental testing significantly raises the likelihood of the discovery of platform-level problems during IOT&E.

• The Navy plans to deliver CVN-78 in February 2016. The ship's post-shipyard shakedown availability will follow delivery in 2016. During the post-shipyard shakedown availability installations of some systems will be completed. The first at-sea operational test and evaluation of CVN-78 will begin in July 2017.

Reliability

• CVN-78 includes several systems that are new to aircraft carriers; four of these systems stand out as being critical to flight operations: EMALS [Electromagnetic Aircraft Launch System], AAG [Advanced Arresting Gear], DBR [Dual Band Radar], and the Advanced Weapons Elevators (AWEs). Overall, the uncertain reliability of these four systems is the most significant risk to the CVN-78 IOT&E. All four of these systems will be tested for the first time in their shipboard configurations aboard CVN-78. Reliability estimates derived from test data are available for EMALS and AAG and are discussed below. For DBR and AWE, estimates based on test data are not available and only engineering reliability estimates are available.

SGR

• It is unlikely that CVN-78 will achieve its SGR requirement. The target threshold is based on unrealistic assumptions including fair weather and unlimited visibility, and that aircraft

---

[24] Letter and attachment from Secretary of the Navy Ray Mabus to Senator John McCain, undated but posted at InsideDefnse.com (subscription required) on March 27, 2012. InsideDefense.com's description of the letter states that it is dated March 26, 2012.

emergencies, failures of shipboard equipment, ship maneuvers (e.g., to avoid land), and manning shortfalls will not affect flight operations. DOT&E plans to assess CVN-78 performance during IOT&E by comparing to the demonstrated performance of the Nimitz class carriers. A demonstrated SGR less than the requirement but equal to or greater than the performance of the Nimitz class could potentially be acceptable.

• During the operational assessment, DOT&E conducted an analysis of past aircraft carrier operations in major conflicts. The analysis concludes that the CVN-78 SGR requirement is well above historical levels and that CVN-78 is unlikely to achieve that requirement. There are concerns with the reliability of key systems that support sortie generation on CVN-78. Poor reliability of these critical systems could cause a cascading series of delays during flight operations that would affect CVN-78's ability to generate sorties, make the ship more vulnerable to attack, or create limitations during routine operations. DOT&E assesses the poor or unknown reliability of these critical subsystems will be the most significant risk to CVN-78's successful completion of IOT&E. The analysis also considered the operational implications of a shortfall and concluded that as long as CVN-78 is able to generate sorties comparable to Nimitz class carriers, the operational implications of CVN-78 will be similar to that of a Nimitz class carrier.[25]

Manning

• Current manning estimates have shortages of bunks for Chief Petty Officers (CPOs) and do not provide the required 10 percent SLA. Per Office of the Chief of Naval Operations Instruction 9640.1B, Shipboard Habitability Program, all new ships are required to have a growth allowance of 10 percent of the ship's company when the ship delivers. The SLA provides empty bunks to allow for changes in the crew composition over CVN-78's expected 50-year lifespan and provides berthing for visitors and Service members temporarily assigned to the ship.

EMALS

• EMALS is one of the four systems critical to flight operations. While testing to date has demonstrated that EMALS should be able to launch aircraft planned for CVN-78's air wing, the system's reliability is uncertain. At the Lakehurst, New Jersey, test site, over 1,967 launches have been conducted and 201 chargeable failures have occurred. Based on available data, the program estimates that EMALS has approximately 240 Mean Cycles Between Critical Failure in the shipboard configuration, where a cycle represents the launch of one aircraft. Based on expected reliability growth, the failure rate is presently five times higher than should be expected.

AAG

• AAG is another system critical to flight operations. Testing to date has demonstrated that AAG should be able to recover aircraft planned for the CVN-78 air wing, but as with EMALS, AAG's reliability is uncertain. At the Lakehurst, New Jersey test site, 71 arrestments were conducted earlier this year and 9 chargeable failures occurred. The Program Office estimates that AAG has approximately 20 Mean Cycles Between Operational Mission Failure in the shipboard configuration, where a cycle represents the recovery of one aircraft. Based on expected reliability growth, the failure rate is presently 248 times higher than should be expected.

---

[25] The issue of the sortie generation rate was also discussed in Tony Capaccio, "Hagel Told New Carrier Unlikely to Meet Aircraft Goals," *Bloomberg News*, January 10, 2014.

DBR

• Previous testing of Navy combat systems similar to CVN-78's revealed numerous integration problems that degrade the performance of the combat system. Many of these problems are expected to exist on CVN-78. The previous results emphasize the necessity of maintaining a DBR/CVN-78 combat system asset at Wallops Island. The Navy is considering long-term plans (i.e., beyond FY15) for testing DBR at Wallops Island, Virginia, but it is not clear if resources and funding will be available. Such plans are critical to delivering a fully-capable combat system and ensuring lifecycle support after CVN-78 delivery in 2016.

JPALS [Joint Precision Approach and Landing System]

• The Navy has proposed to the USD(AT&L) Milestone Decision Authority that the program be restructured from its current, land- and sea-based, multiple-increment structure to a single increment focusing on sea-based requirements primarily supporting JSF [Joint Strike Fighter; aka F-35] and future Unmanned Carrier Launched Airborne Surveillance and Strike aircraft. Under this proposed restructuring scheme, there will be no retrofitting of JPALS on legacy aircraft and the Navy will need to maintain both the legacy approach and landing system and JPALS onboard each aircraft-capable ship.

JSF

• The arresting hook system remains an integration risk as the JSF development schedule leaves no time for discovering new problems. The redesigned tail hook has an increased downward force as well as sharper design that may induce greater than anticipated wear on the flight deck.

• JSF noise levels remain moderate to high risk in JSF integration and will require modifi ed carrier flight deck procedures.

- Flight operations normally locate some flight deck personnel in areas where double hearing protection would be insufficient during F-35 operations. To partially mitigate noise concerns, the Navy will procure new hearing protection with active noise reduction for flight deck personnel.

- Projected noise levels one level below the flight deck (03 level), which includes mission planning spaces, will require at least single hearing protection that will make mission planning difficult. The Navy is working to mitigate the effects of the increased noise levels adjacent to the flight deck.

• Storage of the JSF engine is limited to the hangar bay, which will affect hangar bay operations. The impact on the JSF logistics footprint is not yet known.

• Lightning protection of JSF aircraft while on the flight deck will require the Navy to modify nitrogen carts to increase their capacity. Nitrogen is used to fill fuel tank cavities while aircraft are on the flight deck.

• JSF remains unable to share battle damage assessment and non-traditional Intelligence, Surveillance, and Reconnaissance information captured on the aircraft portable memory device or cockpit voice recorder in real-time. In addition, the CVN-78 remains unable to receive and display imagery transmitted through Link 16 because of bandwidth limitations. These capability gaps were identified in DOT&E's FY12 Annual Report. The Combatant Commanders have requested these capabilities to enhance decision-making.

LFT&E [Live Fire Test and Evaluation]

• While the Navy has made substantial effort in component and surrogate testing, this work does not obviate the need to conduct the FSST [Full Ship Shock Trial] to gain the critical empirical data that past testing has repeatedly demonstrated are required to rigorously evaluate the ship's ability to withstand shock and survive in combat. Shock Trials conducted on both the Nimitz class aircraft carrier and the San Antonio class Amphibious Transport Dock demonstrated the need for and substantial value of conducting the FSST. Postponing the FSST until CVN-79 would cause a five- to seven-year delay in obtaining the data critical to evaluating the survivability of the CVN-78 and would preclude timely modification of subsequent ships of this class to assure their survivability.

• CVN-78 has many new critical systems that have not undergone shock trials on other platforms. Unlike past tests on other new classes of ships with legacy systems, the performance of CVN-78's new critical systems under test is unknown.

• The Navy proposes delaying the shock trial by five to seven years because of the approximately four- to six-month delay required to perform the FSST. The benefit of having test data to affect the design of future carriers in the class outweighs the delay in delivery of CVN-78 to the fleet to conduct this test. The delay is not a sufficient reason to postpone the shock trial.

Recommendations

• Status of Previous Recommendations. The Navy should continue to address the seven remaining FY10 and FY11 recommendations.

1. Adequately test and address integration challenges with JSF; specifically:

- Logistics (unique concerns for storage and transportation)

- Changes required to JBDs [Jet Blast Deflectors]

- Changes to flight deck procedures due to heat and noise

- Autonomic Logistics Information System integration

2. Finalize plans that address CVN-78 Integrated Warfare System engineering and ship's self-defense system discrepancies prior to the start of IOT&E.

3. Continue aggressive EMALS and AAG risk-reduction efforts to maximize opportunity for successful system design and test completion in time to meet required in-yard dates for shipboard installation of components.

4. Continue development of a realistic model for determining CVN-78's SGR, while utilizing realistic assumptions regarding equipment availability, manning, and weather conditions for use in the IOT&E.

5. Provide scheduling, funding, and execution plans to DOT&E for the live SGR test event during the IOT&E.

6. Continue to work with the Navy's Bureau of Personnel to achieve adequate depth and breadth of required personnel to sufficiently meet Navy Enlisted Classification fit/fill manning requirements of CVN-78.

7. Conduct system-of-systems developmental testing to preclude discovery of deficiencies during IOT&E.

• FY13 Recommendations. The Navy should:

1. Address the uncertain reliability of EMALS, AAG, DBR, and AWE. These systems are critical to CVN-78 flight operations, and are the largest risk to the program.

2. Conduct fully integrated, robust, end-to-end testing of the proposed JPALS, to include operations in neutral and potentially hostile electronic warfare environments.[26]

Potential Two-Ship Block Buy on CVN-79 and CVN-80

Another issue for Congress concerns the potential for procuring CVN-79 and CVN-80 together in a two-ship block buy. The Navy currently plans to procure CVN-79 and CVN-80 separately, as one-ship procurements. Procuring the two ships together in a block buy could reduce their combined procurement cost.

Procuring two aircraft carriers together in a two-ship block buy has been done on two previous occasions. The Navy procured two Nimitz (CVN-68) class aircraft carriers (CVN-72 and CVN-73) together in a block buy in FY1983, and procured another two Nimitz-class aircraft carriers (CVN-74 and CVN-75) together in a block buy in FY1988. The Navy proposed these block buys in the FY1983 and FY1988 budget submissions.[27]

When the FY1983 block buy was proposed, the Navy estimated that the block buy would reduce the combined cost of CVN-72 and CVN-73 by 5.6% in real terms.[28] When the FY1988 block buy was proposed, the Navy estimated that the block buy would reduce the combined cost of CVN-74 and CVN-75 by a considerably larger percentage. GAO stated that the savings would be considerably less than the Navy estimated, but agreed that a two-ship acquisition strategy is less expensive than a single-ship acquisition strategy, and that some savings would occur in a two-ship strategy for CVN-74 and CVN-75.[29]

---

[26] Department of Defense, Director, Operational Test & Evaluation, *FY2013 Annual Report*, released January 2014, pp. 157-159. See also Olga Belogolova, "Navy Pushes Back On DOT&E Reliability Concerns For Ford-Class Carrier," *Inside the Navy*, February 24, 2014.

[27] It can also be noted that the Air Force is procuring two Advanced EHF (AEHF) satellites under a two-satellite block buy that the Air Force proposed and Congress approved in FY2012.

[28] See General Accounting Office, *Request to Fully Fund Two Nuclear Aircraft Carriers in Fiscal Year 1983*, MASAD-82-87 (B-206847), March 26, 1982, 10 pp. The figure of 5.6% was derived by dividing $450 million in non-inflation cost avoidance shown on page 5 by the combined estimated cost of the two ships (absent a block buy) of $8,024 million shown on page 4.

[29] See General Accounting Office, Procurement Strategy For Acquiring Two Nuclear Aircraft Carriers, Statement of Frank Conahan, Assistant Comptroller General, National Security and International Affairs Division, Before the Conventional Forces and Alliance Defense Subcommittee and Projection Forces and Regional Defense Subcommittee of the Senate Armed Services Committee, April 7, 1987, T-NSIAD-87-28, 5 pp. The testimony states on page 2 that "A single ship acquisition strategy is more expensive because materials are bought separately for each ship rather than being combined into economic order quantity buys under a multi-ship procurement." The report discounted the Navy's estimated savings of $1,100 million based on this effect on the grounds that if CVN-74 and CVN-75 were not procured in the proposed two-ship block buy, with CVN-74 procured in FY1990 and CVN-75 procured FY1993, it was likely that CVN-74 and CVN-75 would subsequently be procured in a two-ship block buy, with CVN-74 procured in FY1994 and CVN-75 procured in FY1996. For the discussion here, however, the comparison is between the Navy's current plan to procure CVN-79 and CVN-80 separately and the potential alternative of procuring them together in a block buy. (continued...)

The FY1983 and FY1988 block buys each involved procuring two aircraft carriers in a single year. Procuring two carriers in the same year, however, is not mandatory for a two-ship aircraft carrier block buy. The Navy, for example, proposed the block buy for CVN-74 and CVN-75 in the FY1988 budget submission as something that would involve procuring CVN-74 in FY1990 and CVN-75 in FY1993. (Congress, in acting on the FY1988 budget, decided to not only approve the two-ship block buy, but also accelerate the procurement of both CVN-74 and CVN-75 to FY1988.)[30] A block buy on CVN-79 and CVN-80 could leave intact the FY2013 procurement date for CVN-79 and the FY2018 procurement date for CVN-80. This would permit the funding for the two ships to be spread out over the same fiscal years as currently planned, although the amounts of funding in individual years would likely change.

It is too late to implement a complete block buy on CVN-79 and CVN-80, because some of CVN-79, particularly its propulsion plant, has already been purchased. Consequently, the option would be to implement a partial block buy that would include the remaining part of CVN-79 and all of CVN-80.

To illustrate the notional scale of the savings that might result from using a block buy strategy on CVN-79 and CVN-80, it can be noted that if such a block buy were to achieve one-third as much percentage cost reduction as the FY1983 block buy—that is, if it were to reduce the combined procurement cost of CVN 79 and 80 by about 1.9%—that would equate to a savings of roughly $470 million on the currently estimated combined procurement cost of CVN-79 and CVN-80. More refined estimates might be higher or lower than this notional figure of $470 million.

At a March 19, 2012, briefing for CRS and CBO on the CVN-78 program, CRS asked the Navy whether it was considering the possibility of a block buy on CVN-79 and CVN-80. The Navy stated that it had looked into a narrower option of doing joint purchases of some materials for the two ships.

Implementing a block buy on CVN-79 and CVN-80 would require committing to the procurement of CVN-80. Whether Congress would want to commit to the procurement of CVN-80, particularly in light of current uncertainty over future levels of defense spending, is a factor that Congress may consider in assessing the option of doing a block buy. If budgetary circumstances were to lead to a decision to end procurement of Ford-class carriers after CVN-79, then much or all of the funding spent procuring materials for CVN-80 could go to waste.

(...continued)

The GAO report commented on an additional $700 million in savings that the Navy estimated would be derived from improving production continuity between CVN-73, CVN-74, and CVN-75 by stating on page 3 that "It is logical to assume that savings are possible through production continuity but the precise magnitude of such savings is difficult to calculate because of the many variables that affect the outcome." It is not clear how significant savings from production continuity might be in a two-ship block buy for CVN-79 and CVN-80 if the procurement dates for the two ships (FY2013 and FY2018, respectively) are not changed.

The GAO report noted that the Navy estimated $500 million in additional savings from avoided configuration changes on CVN-74 and CVN-75 if the ships were procured in FY1990 and FY1993 rather than FY1994 and FY1996. It is not clear how significant the savings from avoided configuration changes might be for a two-ship block buy for CVN-79 and CVN-80.

See also CRS Issue Brief IB87043, *Aircraft Carriers (Weapons Facts)*, 13 pp., updated February 10, 1988, and archived March 24, 1988, by Ronald O'Rourke. The report includes a discussion of the above GAO report. The report is out of print and available directly from the author.

[30] See CRS Issue Brief IB87043, *Aircraft Carriers (Weapons Facts)*, 13 pp., updated February 10, 1988, and archived March 24, 1988, by Ronald O'Rourke. The report is out of print and available directly from the author.

At a March 29, 2012, hearing on Navy shipbuilding programs before the Seapower and Projection Forces subcommittee of the House Armed Services Committee, Sean Stackley, the Assistant Secretary of the Navy for Research, Development, and Acquisition (i.e., the Navy's acquisition executive), stated the following when asked by Representative Robert Wittman about the possibility of a two-ship block buy on CVN-79 and CVN-80:

> Yes, sir. Let me focus on affordability of the CVN-78 class. We are right now about 40 percent complete construction of the CVN-78 and we're running into some very difficult cost growth issues across the full span—design, material procurement, and production— material procurement on both contractor and government side.
>
> So our first focus right now is to stabilize the lead ship. Let's get cost under control so we can complete this ship as close to schedule at the lowest cost possible.
>
> But in parallel, the Navy is working very closely with the shipbuilder to take a step back and say, one, what are all the lessons we just learned on CVN-78? Two, CVN-78 is a very different ship from the Nimitz [CVN-68]; we cannot expect to build the [CVN-]78 the way we build the [CVN-]68 and—and get to an affordable ship construction plan. So we're pressing on the way the carrier is built—the build plan for the carrier—to arrive at a more affordable CVN-79.
>
> Now, in the process of doing that we'll take a hard look at what opportunity there is across [CVN-]79 and [CVN-]80, recognizing that we're going to be limited, again, by [budget] top line. But there are going to be some opportunities that jump out at us. We don't want to have to replan each carrier. We have a vendor base that is stretched out with the carrier build cycle that for some components that are carrier-unique, that vendor base is—is just struggling to hold on between the five-year gaps.
>
> So we have to take a hard look at where does it make sense after we've gotten to what I'm calling an optimal build plan for CVN-79 and then be able to come back and—and say, OK, here—on CVN-79 here are some opportunities that if we could, in fact, reach out to CVN-80 we can either avoid a gap in a production line or avoid unnecessary cost growth on that follow ship.[31]

Later in the hearing, the following exchange occurred:

> REPRESENTATIVE RICK LARSEN:
>
> Finally, we had some discussion about this question with regard to CVNs and trying to find a way to squeeze some costs out, and one of the ideas was to do some—do block buy of certain components of—of—of CVN components. And have you considered that, and what's your thought on that on block buy on components from [CVN-]79 to [CVN-]80, or whatever, [CVN-]79, [CVN-]79 to [CVN-]80, and so on?
>
> ASSISTANT SECRETARY OF THE NAVY SEAN STACKLEY:
>
> Yes, sir. At this point in time the Navy and the shipbuilder are sitting side by side putting together a build plan for CVN-79. We're 40 percent complete construction of the [CVN-]78; we've got a lot that we've got to, I'll say, do different on the [CVN-]79 and follow from the lead ship. It's a very different ship class [compared to the Nimitz class].

---

[31] Source: transcript of hearing.

So we're taking a hard look at the build plan [for CVN-78]. We need to get that locked down. And associated with that is the complete bill of materials for the Ford class.

At that point in time we'll be able to take a look at...

LARSEN:

On this, call it bill of materials, what does it make sense—what makes sense in terms of looking long term, beyond the immediate ship?

STACKLEY:

Right.

LARSEN:

Are there areas of the industrial base that are stressed to the point that it does make sense to look at coupling the CVN-79 and CVN-80 buy?

STACKLEY:

We're not at that point yet. I described earlier that I think after we get through this build plan review then we'll be able to come back in '14 [FY2014] and identify potential critical items that warrant a block buy approach.[32]

Later in the hearing, Matthew Mulherin, president of NNS and corporate vice president of HII, stated the following when asked by Representative Robert Wittman about the possibility of a two-ship block buy on CVN-79 and CVN-80:

Yes, sir. You know, historically you go back, you were exactly right, if you look at the contracts that bought the CVN- 72 and [CVN-]73 there was huge savings that flowed to the second ship, both in the ability to go buy materials, a block buy and get—get discounts there, but also that you did the engineering up front the first time for both hulls so the second ship you really just had the answer, problem, paper [sic] and some of those kind of things the— the kind of the normal course of business to support the waterfront.

So I wouldn't see any different. I think if we were able to do it both for material, for—for the engineering to be able to go pump out drawings that had two-ship applicability—plus, I think it brings the—the—the CVN—if we were to do a two-ship buy for [CVN-]79 and [CVN-]80 it would ensure CVN-80 was a copy of CVN-79, no change into the contract or very minimal, you're not having a—on the material side you get economic order savings, you don't have to deal with obsolescence.

So absolutely. I think there's huge opportunity to go do that. You know, you talk to the—the vendor base. They would love to see it. It gives them the ability to go look at—at what investments they need, what work is out in front of them, and go invest in—in training and tools to—to be able to go support that.[33]

---

[32] Source: Transcript of hearing.

[33] Source: Transcript of hearing.

At the March 19, 2012, briefing for CRS and CBO on the CVN-78 program, CRS asked the Navy to examine the option of a block buy on CVN-79 and CVN-80, and inform CRS and CBO of the Navy's estimate of how much it might reduce the combined procurement cost of CVN-79 and CVN-80. The Navy's response, dated April 22, 2012, was sent to CRS on May 10, 2012 (i.e., just after the House Armed Services Committee completed its markup of H.R. 4310, the FY2013 National Defense Authorization Act). The response stated:

> There are several options for procuring aircraft carriers that differ from the current practice; two ship buys and block buys. Navy experience with aircraft carrier two ship buys includes procurement of the CVN 72 and CVN 73 (awarded in FY83), and the CVN 74 and CVN 75 (awarded in FY88). The actual cost returns for these procurements support significant savings compared to other NIMITZ Class single ship buys. This conclusion is based on a comparison of the NIMITZ Class two ship buys (CVN72, 73, 74 & 75) with single ship buys (CVN71 and CVN76). The total ship man-hour comparison shows a 9% reduction. The total ship material comparison in constant dollars shows an 8% reduction. The NIMITZ- Class two ship buys took advantage of a single year of full funding for the combined procurement, and less than three years between the deliveries of each ship. Having both ships fully funded in one year enabled the Navy and shipbuilder to take advantage of two ship-set Economic Order Quantity (EOQ) market savings for material items, and also allowed the shipbuilder to optimize production trades management. The short time between deliveries also resulted in design stability, minimized potential obsolescence, and greater opportunities for learning.
>
> Given hard budget constraints in FY13 and FY14, CVN 79 and CVN 80 cannot benefit from a multiyear construct, similar to those requested in PB13 for VIRGINIA Class Submarine and ARLIEGH BURKE Class Destroyers. By the end of FY14, 75% of CVN 79 material will be under contract with suppliers, leaving limited opportunities to implement material savings with multiyear incremental funding. 75% of CVN 80 material would also be incapable of achieving savings, as the material purchases would be placed after CVN 79.
>
> CVN 80/81 would present the first opportunity to potentially consider this strategy.[34]

The Navy's response states, "Having both ships fully funded in one year enabled the Navy and shipbuilder to take advantage of two ship-set Economic Order Quantity (EOQ) market savings for material items.... " It can be noted that ships funded in separate years can also take advantage of EOQ savings, provided that the authorizing legislation permits the use of EOQ, and that the FY1988 block buy of CVN-74 and CVN-75 was originally proposed by the Navy as a block buy in which CVN-74 would be procured in FY1990 and CVN-75 in FY1993.

The Navy's response states, "Given hard budget constraints in FY[20]13 and FY[20]14, CVN 79 and CVN 80 cannot benefit from a multiyear construct, similar to those requested in PB[20]13[35] for VIRGINIA Class Submarine and ARLIEGH BURKE Class Destroyers." It can be noted that a block buy on CVN-79 and CVN-80 would not necessarily be a multiyear procurement (MYP) contract, like those requested for the Virginia-class submarine program and the Arleigh Burke (DDG-51) destroyer programs. It can also be noted that Congress may decide to work within budget constraints for FY2013 and FY2014 that might differ from those on which is DOD basing its planning.

---

[34] Navy information paper dated April 25, 2012, sent to CRS on May 10, 2012.

[35] This is a reference to the President's budget for FY2013—that is, the Administration's requested budget for FY2013.

The Navy's response states, "By the end of FY14, 75% of CVN 79 material will be under contract with suppliers, leaving limited opportunities to implement material savings with multiyear incremental funding. 75% of CVN 80 material would also be incapable of achieving savings, as the material purchases would be placed after CVN 79." CRS on May 10, 2012, asked the Navy what percent of the material for CVN-79 would be under contract by the end of FY2012. The Navy's response, dated May 22, 2012, was sent to CRS on May 25, 2012 (i.e., the same day that the House Appropriations Committee reported H.R. 5856, the FY2013 DOD Appropriations Act). The response stated, "Approximately 47% of CVN 79 direct material will be under contract by the end of FY[20]12."[36]

The Navy's response states that "CVN 80/81 would present the first opportunity to potentially consider this [block buy] strategy." This statement appears to refer to a strategy of a complete block buy involving 100% of the material for both carriers. Based on the Navy's response dated May 22, 2012, a partial block buy on CVN-79 and CVN-80 involving as much as 53% of the material on CVN-79 might be possible, if the block buy were authorized and implemented as part of the FY2013 defense budget.

Legislative Activity for FY2015

FY2015 Funding Request

As shown in **Table 1**, the Navy's proposed FY2014 budget requested $663.0 million in procurement funding to cover cost growth on CVN-78, and $1,300.0 million in procurement funding for CVN-79. The Navy's request for $663.0 million in procurement funding to cover cost growth on CVN-78 forms part of a request for $1,007.3 million in cost-to-complete funding for various prior-year-funded Navy shipbuilding programs.

FY2015 National Defense Authorization Act (H.R. 4435/S. 2410)

House

The House Armed Services Committee, in its report (H.Rept. 113-446 of May 13, 2014) on H.R. 4435, recommends approving the Navy's request for FY2015 procurement funding for the CVN-78 program. (Page 395, line 001, and page 396, line 021).

The report also recommends $483.6 million for the refueling complex overhaul (RCOH) of the aircraft carrier *George Washington* (CVN-73). (Page 395, line 004.) As discussed in **Appendix B**, FY2015 funding for an RCOH for CVN-73 has emerged as an issue in Congress's review of DOD's proposed FY2015 budget.

Section 1024 of H.R. 4435 as reported states:

---

[36] Navy information paper dated May 22, 2012, sent to CRS on May 25, 2012.

SEC. 1024. LIMITATION ON EXPENDITURE OF FUNDS UNTIL COMMENCEMENT OF PLANNING OF REFUELING AND COMPLEX OVERHAUL OF THE U.S.S. GEORGE WASHINGTON.

Not more than 50 percent of the funds authorized to be appropriated or otherwise made available under section 301 of this Act for the Office of the Secretary of Defense for fiscal year 2015 may be obligated or expended until the Secretary of Defense obligates funds to commence the planning and long lead time material procurement associated with the refueling and complex overhaul of the U.S.S. George Washington (CVN-73).

Senate

The Senate Armed Services Committee, in its report (S.Rept. 113-176 of June 2, 2014) on S. 2410, recommends approving the Navy's request for FY2015 procurement funding for the CVN-78 program. (Page 323, line 1, and page 324, line 21).

The report recommends in effect transferring from the Operation and Maintenance, Navy (OMN) account to the Shipbuilding and Conversion, Navy (SCN) account the Navy's request for $46 million in FY2015 funding for defueling the aircraft carrier *George Washington* (CVN-73), so as to support a refueling complex overhaul (RCOH) for that ship. (Page 323, line 04.) As discussed in **Appendix B**, FY2015 funding for an RCOH for CVN-73 has emerged as an issue in Congress's review of DOD's proposed FY2015 budget. Regarding this transfer of funds, S.Rept. 113-176 states:

> **Aircraft carrier defueling planning funds**
>
> The budget request included $46.0 million in the Operation and Maintenance, Navy (OMN) account for advance planning funding for defueling of the USS George Washington (CVN–73) in fiscal year 2017.
>
> It is the committee's intent that the Navy proceed with the refueling and complex overhaul of the USS George Washington (CVN–73) should additional funds be made available in fiscal year 2015 for that purpose.
>
> Therefore, the committee recommends a reduction of $46.0 million in OMN, and an increase of $46.0 million for CVN Refueling Overhauls in the Shipbuilding and Conversion, Navy account. (Page 72)

Section 123 of S. 2410 as reported states:

> SEC. 123. AUTHORITY TO TRANSFER CERTAIN FUNDS FOR REFUELING OF AIRCRAFT CARRIER AND CONSTRUCTION OF AMPHIBIOUS SHIP.
>
> (a) In General- To the extent provided in appropriations Acts, upon a determination described in subsection (b), the Secretary of the Navy is authorized to transfer funds available in Shipbuilding and Conversion, Navy or any other Navy procurement account for either or both of the following purposes:
>
> (1) Up to $650,000,000 to conduct a refueling and complex overhaul of the U.S.S. George Washington (CVN-73).
>
> (2) Up to $650,000,000 for the ship construction of a San Antonio class amphibious ship.

(b) Determination- A determination described in this subsection is a determination by the Secretary of the Navy that--

(1) unobligated balances are available in the program or programs from which funds will be transferred pursuant to subsection (a) due to slower than expected program execution; and

(2) the transfer of funds will fill a high priority military need and is in the best interest of the Department of the Navy.

(c) Contingent Authorization- The Secretary of the Navy is authorized to enter into a contract for the procurement of one San Antonio class amphibious ship beginning in fiscal year 2015, and to use incremental funding for the procurement of that ship, if additional funds are made available for such purpose in fiscal year 2015 and the Secretary determines that such procurement will fill a high priority military need and is in the best interests of the Department of the Navy.

(d) Effect on Authorization Amounts- A transfer made from one account to another under the authority of this section shall be deemed to increase the amount authorized for the account to which the amount is transferred by an amount equal to the amount transferred.

(e) Construction of Authority- The transfer authority under this section is in addition to any other transfer authority provided in this Act.

Regarding Section 123, S.Rept. 113-176 states:

Authority to transfer certain funds for refueling of aircraft carrier and construction of amphibious ship (sec. 123)

The committee recommends a provision that would authorize the Secretary of the Navy to transfer funds available in the Shipbuilding and Conversion, Navy (SCN), or other Navy procurement account for either or both of the following purposes:

(1) Up to $650.0 million to conduct a refueling and complex overhaul of the USS George Washington (CVN–73).

(2) Up to $650.0 million to build a San Antonio-class amphibious ship.

The provision would require that the Secretary make a determination that unobligated balances to be transferred are available due to slower than expected program execution, and the transfer of funds will fill a high priority military need and is in the best interest of the Department of the Navy.

It is the committee's intent that the Navy proceed with the refueling and complex overhaul of the USS George Washington (CVN–73) should additional funds be made available in fiscal year 2015 for that purpose.

Finally, the provision would authorize the Secretary to use incremental funding for a San Antonio-class ship if additional funds are made available in fiscal year 2015 for that purpose and the Secretary determines that such procurement will fill a high priority military need and is in the best interest of the Department of the Navy.

The committee expects that, if the Secretary chooses to transfer funds for the San Antonio-class program in fiscal year 2015, the Secretary will use funds from fiscal year 2015 and fiscal year 2016 to fully fund any new San Antonio-class ship put on contract during fiscal year 2015 or fiscal year 2016. (Pages 8-9)

Section 1021 of S. 2410 as reported states:

SEC. 1021. LIMITATION ON USE OF FUNDS FOR INACTIVATION OF U.S.S. GEORGE WASHINGTON.

No funds authorized to be appropriated by this Act or otherwise made available for fiscal year 2015 for the Navy may be obligated or expended to conduct tasks connected to the inactivation of the U.S.S. George Washington (CVN-73) unless such tasks are identical to tasks that would be necessary to conduct a refueling and complex overhaul of the vessel.

Regarding Section 1021, S.Rept. 113-176 states:

Limitation on use of funds for inactivation of U.S.S. George Washington (sec. 1021)

The committee recommends a provision that would prevent the Navy from obligating or expending any funds in fiscal year 2015 on inactivating the U.S.S. George Washington (CVN–73) unless such obligation or expenditure is to support tasks that are identical to tasks that would be necessary to conduct a refueling complex overhaul (RCOH) of the ship.

The Navy had planned to conduct an RCOH on CVN–73, beginning in fiscal year 2016. The fiscal year 2015 budget request altered that plan to drop the RCOH and inactivate CVN–73. Congress has already authorized and appropriated $329.7 million for the CVN–73 RCOH. The plan for fiscal year 2015 submitted with the fiscal year 2014 budget for the Navy was to request another $491.1 million for advance procurement of the CVN–73 RCOH.

In lieu of the plan, the fiscal year 2015 budget request and the future years defense program (FYDP) supports inactivation of CVN–73. Department of Defense (DOD) officials have stated DOD will defer the decision until 2016 on whether to refuel and maintain CVN–73 or inactivate the ship.

The committee is concerned that DOD submitted a fiscal year 2015 budget request and FYDP that are inconsistent with DOD's stated intent to defer a decision on the refueling, and with the requirement of section 5062(b) of title 10, United States Code, that the Navy maintain 11 operational aircraft carriers.

In testimony, Secretary of Defense Charles Hagel confirmed that 11 carriers are a statutory requirement saying, "We follow the authorization and appropriations direction of Congress. We follow the law." Secretary Hagel explained the dichotomy between an avowed plan to maintain 11 operational aircraft carriers and the FYDP by saying he was waiting for a sign from someone, presumably Congress, that DOD would get the partial relief from the effects of sequestration reflected in the FYDP.

The committee has seen no evidence that the requirement for maintaining 11 operational carriers has diminished. In fact, senior Navy leaders have repeatedly stated the need for 11 carriers as the minimum number required to execute the President's National Military Strategy. Senior military officers have testified that global requirements argue for an even larger number of aircraft carriers. The Commander of U.S. Pacific Command noted that, "Based on the world as it is, about 11 aircraft carriers is just—is just barely making it today."

The aircraft carrier remains the most visible projection of military force abroad and is an effective instrument for shaping the perception of allies and potential foes alike. The committee is concerned that inactivating an aircraft carrier with 20 to 30 years of useful service life remaining is a very inefficient use of defense resources and would be inconsistent with implementing the administration's strategic shift toward the Asia-Pacific region, and such an action would send the wrong signals about our determination to support that shift.

Complying with the letter of this section requires that the administration either submit a budget that supports a fleet with 11 operational aircraft carriers or submit a legislative proposal to amend title 10 to readjust the requirement. The administration has done neither. This provision would ensure that the Navy maintains a path of obligations and expenditures consistent with the statutory requirement to maintain 11 operational aircraft carriers.

The committee directs the Secretary of the Navy to report on the effect on capabilities for power projection and global engagement, as it affects the Navy's ability to meet the Defense Strategic Guidance, moving to a permanent force structure of fewer than 11 operational carriers. This report should include a classified annex that describes the Navy's ability to meet the combatant commanders' requirements, both at the current force level and the impact of a force level with fewer than the required 11 operational carriers. This report should also specify what the effects of such action would be on operational deployments, overall readiness, and on sailors and their families. The report should identify potential effects on the shipbuilding industrial base, on the remainder of the RCOH program, on other shipbuilding programs, and on other acquisition programs. The Secretary of the Navy should submit that report with the fiscal year 2016 budget request. (Pages 164-165)

Appendix A. March 2013 Navy Report to Congress on Construction Plan for CVN-79

This appendix reprints a March 2013 Navy report to Congress on the Navy's construction plan for CVN-79.[37]

---

[37] *Aircraft Carrier Construction, John F Kennedy (CVN 79), Report to Congress*, March 2013, 17 pp. An annotation on the report's cover page indicates that the report was authorized for public release on May 16, 2013. The report was posted at InsideDefense.com (subscription required) on June 21, 2013. See also Megan Eckstein, "Navy Plan To Congress Outlines New Strategies To Save On CVN-79," *Inside the Navy*, June 24, 2013.

AIRCRAFT CARRIER CONSTRUCTION
JOHN F KENNEDY (CVN 79)
Report to Congress
March 2013

> The estimated cost of report or study for the
> Department of Defense is approximately
> $13,000.00. This includes $0.00 in expenses
> and $13,000.00 in DoD labor.

FOR OFFICIAL USE ONLY
This document contains information EXEMPT FROM PUBLIC DISCLOSURE under FOIA
Exemption 4 applies

PUBLIC RELEASE
AUTHORIZED ON MAY 16, 2013

Enclosure 2

AIRCRAFT CARRIER CONSTRUCTION
JOHN F KENNEDY (CVN 79)
Report to Congress

The National Defense Authorization Act for FY 2013, Public Law 112-239 contained specific language regarding acquisition of the JOHN F KENNEDY (CVN 79). The language follows:

SEC. 124. LIMITATION ON AVAILABILITY OF AMOUNTS FOR SECOND FORD CLASS AIRCRAFT CARRIER.

(a) LIMITATION.-Of the funds authorized to be appropriated or otherwise made available for fiscal year 2013 for shipbuilding and conversion for the second Ford class aircraft carrier, not more than 50 percent may be obligated or expended until the Secretary of the Navy submits to the congressional defense committees a report setting forth a description of the program management and cost control measures that will be employed in constructing the second Ford class aircraft carrier.

(b) ELEMENTS.-The report described in subsection (a) shall include a plan with respect to the Ford class aircraft carriers to-

(1) maximize planned work in shops and early stages of construction;
(2) sequence construction of structural units to maximize the effects of lessons learned;
(3) incorporate design changes to improve producibility for the Ford class aircraft carriers;
(4) increase the size of erection units to eliminate disruptive unit breaks and improve unit alignment and fairness;
(5) increase outfitting levels for assembled units before erection in the drydock;
(6) increase overall ship completion levels at each key construction event;
(7) improve facilities in a manner that will lead to improved productivity; and
(8) ensure the shipbuilder initiates plans that will improve productivity through capital improvements that would provide targeted return on investment, including-

(A) increasing the amount of temporary and permanent covered work areas;
(B) adding ramps and service towers for improved access to work sites and the drydock; and
(C) increasing lift capacity to enable construction of larger, more fully outfitted superlifts.

This document constitutes the report requested by Congress.

FOR OFFICIAL USE ONLY

This document contains information EXEMPT FROM PUBLIC DISCLOSURE under FOIA Exemption 4 applies

2

Enclosure 2

Executive Summary

The GERALD R FORD (CVN 78) Class, the first new aircraft carrier design in over 40 years, represents a quantum advance in operational capability, survivability, and flexibility to accommodate future improvements in technology and war fighting capability over a 50-year service life, all while lowering total ownership costs by $4B when compared to the standard-bearing NIMITZ class. However, the scope of the CVN 78 "clean sheet" design, which touched virtually every element of the ship has presented challenges to the designer, supplier and shipbuilder for the lead ship both in terms of cost and schedule. The scope and volume of first of class issues on CVN 78 has been the primary factor driving growth in ship construction cost and schedule performance.

As a result of the lessons learned on CVN 78, the approach to carrier construction has undergone an extensive affordability review and the Navy and the shipbuilder have made significant changes on CVN 79 that will significantly reduce the cost to build the ship. These include four key construction areas:

- CVN 79 construction will start with a complete design and a complete bill of material
- CVN 79 construction will start with a firm set of stable requirements
- CVN 79 construction will start with the development complete on a host of new technologies inserted on CVN 78 ranging from the Electromagnetic Aircraft Launch System (EMALS), the Dual Band Radar, and the reactor plant, to key valves in systems throughout the ship
- CVN 79 construction will start with an 'optimal build' plan that emphasizes the completion of work and ship outfitting as early as possible in the construction process to optimize cost and ultimately schedule performance.

In addition to these fundamentals, the Navy and the shipbuilder are tackling cost through a series of other changes that when taken over the entire carrier will have a significant impact on construction costs. The Navy has also imposed cost targets and is aggressively pursuing cost reduction initiatives in its government furnished systems. A detailed accounting of these actions is included in this report.

The actions discussed in this report are expected to reduce the material cost of CVN 79 by 10-20% in real terms from CVN 78, to reduce the number of man-hours required to build the CVN 79 by 15-25% from CVN 78, and to reduce the cost of government furnished systems by 5-10% in real terms from CVN 78. The following table provides an executive summary of the cost reductions anticipated in the key focus areas described in this report.

FOR OFFICIAL USE ONLY

This document contains information EXEMPT FROM PUBLIC DISCLOSURE under FOIA Exemption 4 applies

3

Enclosure 2

Focus Area	Anticipated reduction from CVN 78 to CVN 79
Improvements in material availability and pricing	10-20% in material cost
Major changes in build strategy and processes	10-15% in man-hours to build ship
Design changes for greater producibility	5-10% in man-hours to build ship
Government furnished equipment	5-10% in system costs

Detailed Discussion

IMPROVEMENTS IN MATERIAL AVAILABILITY AND PRICING
(10-20% Reduction in material cost)

As previously discussed, many of the first in class issues experienced during construction of CVN 78 were driven by material availability, vendor qualifications, and material costs. A completed Class design enables the shipbuilder to fully understand the whole ship bill of materials for CVN 79 construction and more effectively manage the procurement of those materials with the knowledge of material lead times and qualified sources accrued from CVN 78 construction. The myriad of vendor first article testing and certification issues which contributed to delays in material delivery on CVN 78 should not recur for CVN 79. The shipbuilder is able to order complete ship-set quantities of material, with attendant cost benefits, and to ensure CVN 79 material will arrive on time to support construction need. Extensive improvements have been put in place for CVN 79 material procurement to drive both cost reductions associated with more efficient procurement strategies and production labor improvements associated with improved material availability. The improved procurement strategies being employed on CVN 79 are expected to yield in real terms a material cost reduction as compared to the CVN 78 of 10-20%. Improved material availability is also a critical enabler to many construction efficiency improvements in CVN 79 discussed later in this report.

In order to maximize material availability and minimize material costs the shipbuilder has developed an entirely new material management strategy for CVN 79. This new strategy consists of eight separate initiatives:

a. **Define the "whole ship" bill of material** - This allows the shipbuilder to maximize opportunities for economic order quantity buy of material items from sub vendors. Reduced material costs will be realized and procurement effort is reduced – with an estimated 30% reduction in total number of purchase order lines as compared with CVN 78.
b. **Establish a "ship view" of equipment by supplier to help incentivize suppliers and correlate supplier priorities based on construction progress and need** - Some sub vendors produce multiple types of components in different geographic locations. Grouping orders by component type and sub vendor subdivision and location helps the shipbuilder define and communicate material priorities to the sub vendor across his enterprise, thereby improving material availability and reducing cost. This also reduces shipbuilder procurement support effort.

FOR OFFICIAL USE ONLY

This document contains information EXEMPT FROM PUBLIC DISCLOSURE under FOIA Exemption 4 applies

4   Enclosure 2

c. **Accelerated production cost avoidance** - The shipbuilder has identified key components that can be purchased earlier than just-in-time construction need, allowing suppliers to level load their production lines and avoid incurring fees for accelerated production.

d. **Multi-ship material buys to leverage economic order quantity pricing** - The shipbuilder is investigating opportunities to procure parts common to multiple ship programs (e.g. CVN 79, Virginia Class Submarines, NIMITZ Class Refueling Complex Overhaul) in a grouped manner to leverage better pricing for all programs. This concept could further be expanded to pursue grouped procurement of material for more than one FORD Class carrier at a time (such as CVN 80 and CVN 81).

e. **Improved material ordering schedule** - Development of, and management to, a comprehensive material procurement plan that considers construction, sequencing, timing, and most recent experience with vendor procurement lead time to schedule a bundled or combined procurement to ensure material is available at the first instance of use.

f. **Soliciting and implementing vendor cost reduction ideas** - The shipbuilder is working with its suppliers to identify cost reduction ideas that may simplify material production and reduce procurement cost. An example is encouraging vendors to recommend changes to ship specification requirements to achieve technical equivalency at reduced cost.

g. **Leveraging supplier competition for cost avoidance** - An example is developing competition for steel supply by establishing a new supplier/source for non-armor steel plate.

h. **Procuring commodity equipment from the original equipment manufacturer** - In many cases the shipbuilder can bulk order commodity equipment for a lower price than an individual sub vendor due to a larger order quantity. The shipbuilder would then provide the commodity material back to the sub vendor to assemble into the finished product at a lower cost. An example would be bundled procurement of motor controllers at a reduced price, some of which would then be provided to a system manufacturer such as the provider of air conditioning plants.

The shipbuilder has undertaken these initiatives in a multi-faceted approach with the objective of driving material cost down, and material availability up to support an optimized construction schedule, within the constraints of the funding available for each fiscal year. In addition the shipbuilder has an ongoing process to inventory all excess material procured on CVN 78 for transfer to CVN 79.

The Navy has also employed outside supply chain management experts to help develop additional optimal CFE material procurement strategies. Furthermore, the Navy has increased its oversight of contractor furnished material procurement, ensuring that material procurement is competed (where competition is available); that it is fixed priced; that commodities are bundled to leverage economic order quantities; and that the vendor base capacity and schedule for receipt supports the optimal build plan being developed for production of CVN 79. The increased oversight has included visits to several key vendors to ensure a deeper, first hand understanding of cost drivers and issues.

FOR OFFICIAL USE ONLY

This document contains information EXEMPT FROM PUBLIC DISCLOSURE under FOIA Exemption 4 applies

5   Enclosure 2

MAJOR CHANGES IN BUILD STRATEGY AND PROCESSES
(10-15% Reduction in man-hours to build ship)

The shipbuilder and the Navy have performed a comprehensive review of the build strategy and processes used in construction of Ford Class aircraft carriers as well as consulted with other Navy shipbuilders on best practices. As a result, the shipbuilder has identified and is implementing a number of changes in the way they build aircraft carriers, with a determined focus on executing construction activities where they can most efficiently be performed. This tends to result in moving production effort earlier in the value stream and in grouping similar work to enhance the effects of learning. Improved material availability as discussed above is a critical element to the success of this approach. The major changes in build strategy and process described below and being employed on CVN 79 are expected to yield a man-hour reduction as compared to the CVN 78 of 10-15%.

1. Maximizing planned work in shops and early stages of construction

Ship construction is most efficiently performed in a shop environment due to ease of access, lifting and handling gear, and environmental controls. The goal for CVN 79 is a 30% increase in front end shop work as compared to CVN 78. This work will result in an increase in pre-outfitting and work pulled to an earlier point in the construction process. It can be broken into two different measureable categories:

a. Work that was originally planned to be performed in the shop on CVN 78, but was deferred due to late material, design maturity, etc. Implementation of lessons learned, a mature design, whole ship bill of materials ordering and more timely delivery of CFE all enable this work to be moved back into the shops on CVN 79 as part of the optimal build strategy.

b. Work that was originally planned in the drydock on CVN 78 that will be moved to an earlier stage of construction for CVN 79 as an improvement to the optimal build strategy. CVN 79 superlift reviews are ongoing to determine what outfitting work should be moved earlier in the construction process. The results of this continuing effort will move a significant amount of work from the drydock back into the platen area (area where module assembly occurs) or the shops.

As part of this strategy, the shipbuilder has begun the shop construction of complex assemblies. These are assemblies of piping, valves, pumps, etc., that would previously have been 'stick built' on the final assembly platen or on the ship. Building these assemblies in a shop environment is far more efficient, allows shop testing and painting currently being done on the platen or ship to be done in the shop environment, and optimizes the eventual transportation of the complex assembly to the ship. The ship design is being reviewed to identify candidates for this complex assembly process with an expectation that over 1,000 assemblies could be shop built shifting hundreds of thousands of hours of work into more efficient shop construction areas. As an example, the first of these assemblies moved to the shop for CVN 79 are fire pumps. On CVN 78, fitting out a fire

FOR OFFICIAL USE ONLY

This document contains information EXEMPT FROM PUBLIC DISCLOSURE under FOIA Exemption 4 applies

6   Enclosure 2

pump room consisted of stick building multiple pumps, valves, actuators, pipe details, and foundations (approximately 250 pieces of material) in a constrained shipboard environment. The goal on CVN 79 is to build out the pump room as a complex assembly in the shop and then land, install, and connect the complex assembly as a single unit into the ship (see figure below).

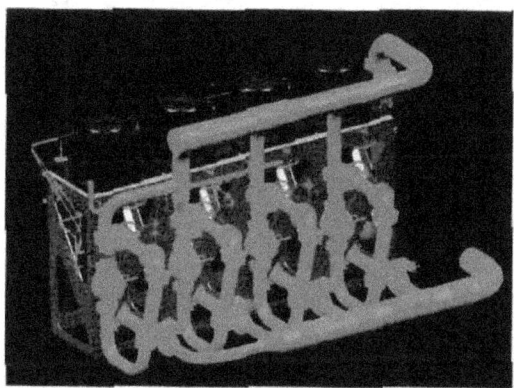

Example of Complex Assembly – Fire Pumps

2. Sequence construction of structural units to maximize the effects of lessons learned

The shipbuilder has developed a 'family of units' concept to maximize the effects of lessons learned within construction of CVN 79 (in addition to lessons learned from construction of CVN 78). This concept is enabled on CVN 79 by the level of design completion and material availability present at the start of ship's construction. Currently, structural units are built in numerous locations and are sequenced to support the ship's schedule, not to best utilize the structural shop footprint and resources. By building units in families, the ship's schedule will still be met, but the structural shop will be better able to shop-load their limited footprint, better utilize equipment, and better assign skilled resources.

The family of units concept allows two distinct execution methods. First, units of a similar construction are set up into flow lanes such that the unit is moved from station to station as various repeated work items are completed, very similar in concept to an assembly line of large components. This concept allows workers to perform repeated tasks on similar units, maximizing learning within a work cell. Unit family production reduces set-up time between units because the jigs and fixtures which support the unit and/or facilitate its construction do not have to be set up again until a new unit family is started. In addition, by organizing into an assembly line process structure, many of the 'lean manufacturing' assembly line controls can be implemented further increasing the efficiency of the process.

FOR OFFICIAL USE ONLY

This document contains information EXEMPT FROM PUBLIC DISCLOSURE under FOIA Exemption 4 applies

7   Enclosure 2

Some structural units in CVN construction are too large to be efficiently moved in an assembly line fashion, but have similar construction methodologies. In these cases, the shipbuilder has established a process where a work cell of individuals is moved from unit to unit to accomplish the same repeatable work in a unit's build cycle, thereby maximizing the learning curve within the individual work cells. Many of the same benefits of the flow lane concept will be realized via this methodology as well.

3. Increase outfitting levels for assembled units before erection in the drydock

Pre-outfitting is a key element for driving cost out of ship construction. This occurs prior to ship erection or ship launch. Installation efficiency increases and construction costs are reduced the earlier in production that piping, valves, ventilation, foundations, cabling, and other outfitting type items can be installed. This plan offers several advantages from easier installation access, to improved trade coordination, to the ability to load more complete assemblies into each unit prior to erection.

The shipbuilder has formed a team consisting of construction, planning, engineering and government personnel to challenge every item installed (or planned to be installed) in the dry-dock or after launch on CVN 78, and to incorporate all lessons learned into the build plan for CVN 79. To date these reviews have resulted in 12% of pipe and ventilation items in the units (totaling about 200 thousand hours) assessed being moved back to the pre-outfitting period on the final assembly platen or in the shop. The shipbuilder also expects to achieve improved performance in pre-outfitting by improving material availability.

4. Increase overall ship completion levels at each key construction event

Fundamental changes to the build processes for CVN 79 and beyond, as described in the preceding paragraphs, are all designed to support accomplishment of work in a more efficient manner and lead to increased overall ship completion levels at each key construction event. The following paragraphs describe additional affordability initiatives being implemented that also facilitate this key focus area:

a. **Batch manufacturing** - An additional benefit of the completed ship design is that the shipbuilder is able to plan for ship set quantity batched production of like items that are used in construction of the ship. The batched production leads to increased efficiency and decreased cost through reductions in planning, production control, material movement, and set up/ tear down times. An example of this is filter housings that are installed in the ship's ventilation system. A filter housing is a relatively simple structure that is inserted into ventilation ducting to retain an air filter. With the class design completed the shipbuilder has an exact requirement for the type and quantity of filter housings needed and can set up small assembly lines to produce these efficiently, whereas on CVN 78 many of these housings were built on

FOR OFFICIAL USE ONLY

This document contains information EXEMPT FROM PUBLIC DISCLOSURE under FOIA
Exemption 4 applies

8   Enclosure 2

an as needed basis as the design developed. The total number of work packages for CVN 79 filter housings will be reduced from 88 to 10.

b. **Common Integrated Work Package** - One of the areas the shipbuilder is implementing to drive production costs out of CVN 79 is the common integrated work package. In the current state multiple work packages are developed to construct a single portion of the ship, there may be design, engineering, and production work packages that are all used to describe the assembly process. This system forces many handoffs between the various departments within the shipyard, increasing the likelihood of inefficiency, transcription errors, and production problems. The goal of integrating the various work packages into a common document is to provide the shipyard mechanic doing the actual work the information they need in a user-friendly, producible format to improve first time quality, overall productivity, innovation and job knowledge capture and transfer.

c. **Flexible Infrastructure** - Flexible infrastructure is rapidly-reconfigurable, modular open systems and standards used in the design and construction of ship's spaces. It facilitates equipment installation, reconfiguration, technology insertion, and improved mission flexibility, while decreasing acquisition and life cycle costs. Flexible infrastructure, including flexible decking, overhead, and bulkhead mounting elements are being employed in the combat systems spaces in the FORD Class design. The shipbuilder is currently studying areas where flexible infrastructure for bulkhead installation of items such as electrical panels can be used in other areas of the ship to drive out construction costs.

d. **Improved cable installation** - The FORD Class design has substantially more electrical cable than NIMITZ Class carriers (9.1M feet for CVN 78 versus 5.5M feet for CVN 77). The shipbuilder is working to improve the various processes associated with cable installation to allow as much cable as possible to be installed at each phase of construction. This includes employing additional analysis to accurately identify cabling with routes wholly contained within units or superlifts to ensure cable installation on platen. Also, analysis is being done to identify logical candidates for "coil and stow" options for cables runs not wholly confined to a unit or superlift. This would allow installation of much of the cable, with the portion crossing the erection break being coiled up and stowed for final installation after erecting the unit. The shipbuilder is also leveraging efforts to improve material availability and increase pre-outfitting of items such as hangers, shell-banks, and wireways to increase the amount of cable that can be installed during each phase of construction.

e. **Pre-outfitting panels** - Steel bulkhead panels and decks are currently fabricated in the shop and then assembled to create units and superlifts. Once they are welded in place, holes are cut in the bulkheads and decks to install a wide variety of components such as coamings, penetrations and hangers. This requires hotwork on the ship, which is accomplished in a poor ergonomic work condition and impacts the start of outfitting. Pre-outfitting bulkheads and decks with these items before they are assembled into units and decks will allow the

FOR OFFICIAL USE ONLY

This document contains information EXEMPT FROM PUBLIC DISCLOSURE under FOIA Exemption 4 applies

9   Enclosure 2

work to be accomplished in a shop environment, instead of on the ship, and will significantly improve the shipbuilder's ability to start outfitting work earlier.

f. **Further advancing CVN construction** - There is a steady strain on identification and implementation of producibility enhancements targeted for CVN 79. There are also some additional initiatives under consideration whose developmental timelines or infrastructure requirements preclude implementation on CVN 79, but are expected to yield marked shipbuilder construction cost reductions for CVN80 and follow FORD Class ships. An example is the Vertical Build Methodology - a methodology which will achieve full potential for shipbuilding cost reduction in CVN 80 and follow ships. When fully implemented, the Vertical Build Methodology will erect the ship in vertical sections thereby allowing easier access for installation of systems, components, equipment, and complex assemblies into the erection units which comprise each vertical section. When the vertical sections are complete, they will be "slid" together to complete assembly of the ship. The graphic below illustrates the concepts of Vertical Build Methodology.

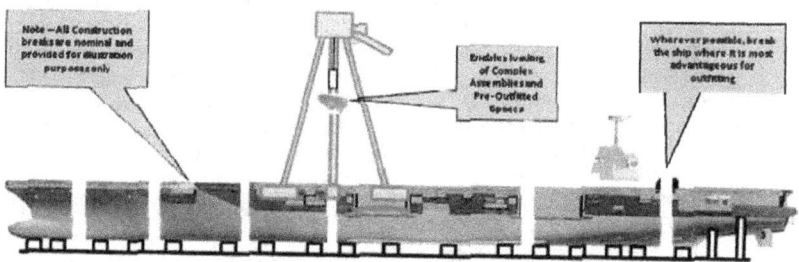

Vertical Build Methodology

Overall, the efforts described in the preceding sections and above serve to move more work into the areas in which it can be most efficiently performed. For CVN 79 construction, an aggressive target has been established to increase the percent complete at launch above that of the CVN 78. The following table shows the planned increase in front end shop and platen work for CVN 79 construction.

Manufacturing & Assembly		
SFA	**CFA**	**FAP**
5-10%	20-30%	5-10%
SFA = Steel Fabrication and Assembly		
CFA = Component Fabrication and Assembly		
FAP = Final Assembly Platen		

Estimated Increase in CVN 79 Front End Work

FOR OFFICIAL USE ONLY

This document contains information EXEMPT FROM PUBLIC DISCLOSURE under FOIA
Exemption 4 applies

10   Enclosure 2

DESIGN CHANGES FOR GREATER PRODUCIBILITY
(5-10% Reduction in man-hours to build ship)

In conjunction with the Navy and the shipbuilder's comprehensive review of the build strategy and processes used in construction of Ford Class aircraft carriers a number of design changes were identified that would result in more affordable construction. Some of these design changes were derived from lessons learned in the construction of CVN 78 and others seek to further simplify the construction process and drive cost down. The design changes described below and being employed on CVN 79 are expected to yield a man-hour reduction as compared to the CVN 78 of 5-10%.

1. Incorporate design changes to improve producibility for FORD Class aircraft carriers

The completion of the FORD Class design and ongoing construction experience on CVN 78 has allowed the shipbuilder to examine ways to improve the producibility of CVN 79. As a part of the design rollover from CVN 78 to CVN 79, shipbuilder design engineers are identifying specific improvements based on these lessons learned to reduce the cost of CVN 79.

One such example addresses CVN 78 producibility problems stemming from the use of thinner plate scantling decks and bulkheads as compared with those of NIMITZ Class. Thinner, lighter weight plate was selected as part of a design objective to reduce overall ship weight and restore growth margin in the ship's lifecycle – a KPP for the ship class. Use of the thinner steel plate has necessitated unplanned use of temporary bracing, as shown in the illustration below, to allow handling of modules during assembly as well as causing rework to flame straighten plates. While a normal evolution in shipbuilding, a greater degree of flame-straightening has been required on CVN 78. The thinner steel plate has also required additional work and structural reinforcement associated with some large heavy component and equipment foundations to achieve proper fit up. Light scantlings also detract from greater outfitting prior to module erection without incurring further deformation. The thinner plate has caused nearly twice the hours in installing temporary bracing and supports as compared to the CVN 77, and incurred indirect additional rigging costs associated with the added difficulty in moving and erecting units. The interference of the temporary bracing is also delaying planned elements of pre-outfitting from being installed on platen.

A multitude of efforts will be utilized on CVN 79 and future hulls to mitigate these disruptions to include: increased thicknesses of platforms and decks, redesigned elevator trunks reducing welding volume and parts, optimized temporary backing structure during lifting and handling, and improved straightening methods (induction heating). These changes will also enable increased pre-outfitting and joining of construction units to build more and larger superlift modules which will reduce the number of erectable modules and improve outfitting of those units. The additional weight associated with these changes can be accommodated within the design margin reserve such that the class KPP for weight service life allowance will still be met.

FOR OFFICIAL USE ONLY

This document contains information EXEMPT FROM PUBLIC DISCLOSURE under FOIA
Exemption 4 applies

11   Enclosure 2

Example of Temporary Bracing Required During Erection Due to Thin Scantling

Another example of design changes improving producibility is associated with a seawater piping system. The original ship design called for a 3 degree bend in a particular pipe to route it around an obstruction. When construction trades tried to produce this section of piping on CVN 78, they found the 3 degree bend extraordinarily hard to produce and properly fit into the piping assembly. Upon completion of the work, the shop foreman suggested the particular piping run be extended by two inches so that a more typical 45 degree piping bend could be inserted into the system. This suggestion is incorporated into the CVN 79 design, making it more producible. In another example, some of the seawater inlets on CVN 78 were produced via a casting process, which resulted in some downstream manufacturing challenges. For CVN 79, the shipbuilder is now producing these seawater inlets via a forging process which has resulted in a more efficient production of this component.

In addition to making design changes to address producibility issues encountered on CVN 78, the CVN 79 design is being reviewed for opportunities to drive out further cost through producibility enhancing design changes. One such opportunity being exploited on CVN 79 is in reducing the number of welded fittings required in the ship's piping systems. Below is a graphic which highlights this concept.

FOR OFFICIAL USE ONLY

This document contains information EXEMPT FROM PUBLIC DISCLOSURE under FOIA
Exemption 4 applies

12   Enclosure 2

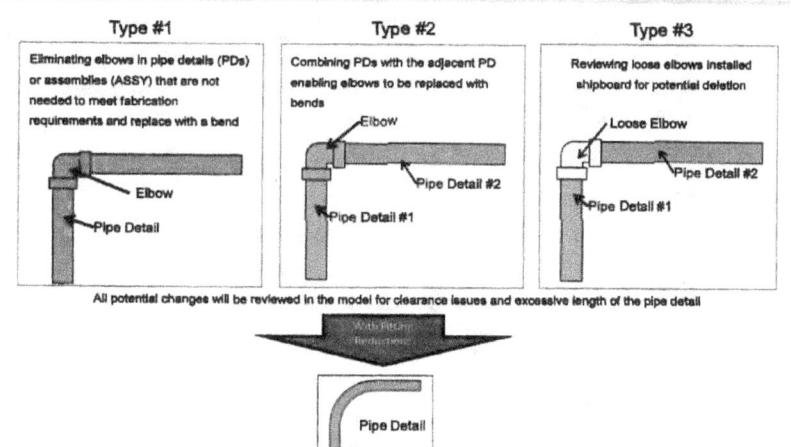

Illustration of Fitting Elimination Concept

Due to the incompleteness of the design during initial construction of CVN 78, many piping systems were built with temporary terminations, with a fitting added later to complete the piping as the follow on compartment was designed/built out. Now that the class design is complete, the shipbuilder is examining where fittings were used in piping systems with the goal of removing as many as possible by replacing the fitting with a bend. To date, more than 30 percent of the total number of elbows has been evaluated, with nearly 2,000 elbows being eliminated from the design, which in turn eliminates nearly 4,000 welds and reduces construction hours by 6 hours per joint on average. Each fitting eliminated removes the requirement for procuring and tracking the fitting as well as for performing two welds and a broad range of production activities.

Shipbuilder producibility reviews are not limited to the outfitting areas, but include structural and welding areas. As shown in the below graphic illustrating a portion of the island, 56 ft of butt weld joint is eliminated from this one area by simply extending thicker plate. There are numerous opportunities like this throughout the ship. These types of seemingly simple ideas when taken over the entire carrier have a significant impact on construction manhours and costs.

FOR OFFICIAL USE ONLY

This document contains information EXEMPT FROM PUBLIC DISCLOSURE under FOIA
Exemption 4 applies

13   Enclosure 2

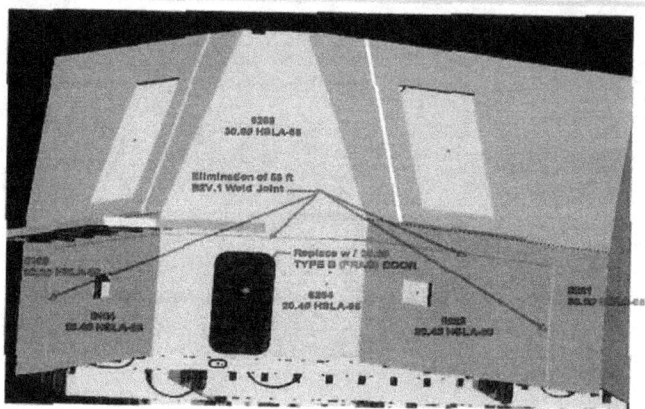

Illustration of Welding Reduction Studies Using 3D Product Model

2. Increasing the size of erection units to eliminate disruptive unit breaks and improve unit alignment and fairness

A completed class design allows the shipbuilder to evaluate the placement of 'construction breaks' between units that will eventually be erected into the drydock. In an ideal scenario, these construction breaks are minimized to allow for additional outfitting of material into construction units during preassembly and on the platen prior to their erection into the drydock. In reality, construction breaks are forced into construction by realistic limits on how much of a unit module can be transported around the shipyard and the weight of a unit module that can be lifted by the gantry crane into the drydock. However, on CVN 78, more construction breaks were used in the original design because of unknowns associated with the first of class build than were actually needed. For CVN 79, the shipbuilder has reduced the number of construction breaks by approximately 5% to allow piping, cabling and ventilation trunks to be extended to the maximum extent feasible. These efforts are raising the level of pre-outfitting on CVN 79 well above that for CVN 78.

As part of the study to remove unnecessary construction breaks from the design, the shipbuilder is evaluating where previously first and final erectable units can be combined onto existing superlifts or combined together to create new superlifts. Creating new superlifts has multiple benefits. A superlift is built from multiple smaller units, and contains piping, machinery, electrical, and ventilation. Each new superlift thus lowers the number of units that need to be independently erected into the drydock, helping to alleviate demands on the gantry drydock crane and decreasing the number of times welders have to work in a constrained environment to weld construction units into the ship. Superlifts allow for more pre-outfitting on the final assembly platen and shops, prior to ship erection, thereby increasing ship construction efficiency.

FOR OFFICIAL USE ONLY

This document contains information EXEMPT FROM PUBLIC DISCLOSURE under FOIA
Exemption 4 applies

14   Enclosure 2

CVN 79 superlift reviews are ongoing and will continue. To date, the shipbuilder has decreased the number of erectable units from CVN 78 by 20 –nearly a 5% reduction. Decreasing the number of erectable units has multiple benefits including reducing the number of lifts required by the 1,050 ton crane – a natural bottleneck in the CVN construction process. Fewer erectable units also reduces the number of unit breaks between sections thereby allowing additional outfitting and improving unit alignment and fairness.

FACILITIES

In addition to the material procurement improvements, build strategy and construction process changes, and design changes described in the preceding sections, the shipbuilder is evaluating capital improvements to facilities that would serve to reduce risk and improve productivity.

Improve facilities in a manner that will lead to improved productivity; and ensure the shipbuilder initiates plans that will improve productivity through capital improvements that would provide targeted return on investment

The shipbuilder is considering what additional facilities, or modifications to existing facilities could be employed to further enhance efficient manufacturing and construction. The shipbuilder has developed a plan to renovate existing facilities to support shop manufacture and assembly of small complex assemblies as well as building a new facility to accomplish the same for large complex assemblies. Additional facilities are also being considered for pre-outfitting structural panels and decks and possibly for increasing the covered work areas on the Final Assembly Platen. Due to the amount of welding involved in carrier construction, the shipbuilder continues to add to its mechanized welding capability.

The shipbuilder is studying capital investment opportunities that could result in reduced risk and additional cost reductions for CVN 79 and/or follow ships in the class. Some initiatives include:

a. **Increasing the Amount of Temporary and Permanent Covered Work Areas** - The shipbuilder has identified the need to increase the amount of covered workspace for the construction of CVN 79. This supports build strategy changes that will move significant outfitting work from the ship to the final assembly platen. These facilities could include both permanent and temporary (moveable) structures. This would include a facility for pre-outfitting structural panels and decks before they are used to build units and superlifts. A recent improvement was made where the shipbuilder tripled the amount of space they had available for blast and coat of assembly units by building two additional blast and coat facilities.

b. **Adding Ramps and Service Towers for Improved Access to Work Sites and the Drydock** - The shipbuilder has added a drydock elevator to allow easier access to drydock num-

FOR OFFICIAL USE ONLY

~~This document contains information~~ EXEMPT ~~FROM PUBLIC DISCLOSURE~~ under FOIA
~~Exemption 4 applies~~

15   Enclosure 2

ber 12. This addition was done toward the later stages of CVN 78 drydock construction and therefore had limited benefit for CVN 78, but is expected to increase the efficiency of movement of material into the drydock for CVN 79 and alleviate the bottleneck imposed by the limited number of lifting cranes. Additional ramps and elevators could further improve the movement of material from material laydown areas to the ship as well as reducing the number of required crane lifts.

c. **Increasing Lift Capacity to Enable Construction of Larger, More Fully Outfitted Superlifts** - Prior to construction of CVN 78, the lifting capacity of the gantry crane used to erect superlifts was increased from 900 to 1050 tons. While this upgrade did show some benefit on CVN 78, many of the superlifts for CVN 78 were not able to fully utilize the capacity increase due to the incompleteness of the design. With the class design complete and the true weight of erectables determined, the shipbuilder is able to plan more efficient combinations of erectables into superlifts to allow for fuller utilization of this increased capacity.

GOVERNMENT FURNISHED EQUIPMENT (GFE)
(5-10% Reduction in GFE cost)

In addition to the substantial improvements being implemented to address shipbuilder costs, aggressive measures have been put in place for cost control in GFE. Recurring engagement and review at the Flag Officer level between Program Executive Officer Aircraft Carriers (PEO CV) and those executives responsible for providing GFE to CVN 79 establishes and maintains the framework in which this occurs.

a. **"Will Cost" / "Should Cost" Management** – For providers of platform GFE (non-reactor plant GFE), "should cost" targets are established at the system level. Specific initiatives to drive cost out of the GFE systems, as well as timelines for realization of the savings for each of the initiatives, are identified and captured on scorecards. These scorecards are evaluated and reviewed between the CVN 79 Program Office and the GFE providers on a routine, recurring basis to ensure actions are on track realize the identified cost reduction opportunities and to identify additional opportunities. Examples of these opportunities include: bundling of procurements with other ship programs, refurbishment of assets recovered from decommissioning ships in lieu of procurement of new assets, reductions in projected systems engineering and installation support based on anticipated lessons learned from CVN 78 installations, and continued or expanded use of fixed price production contracts where appropriate.

b. **Ship Project Directives** – Detailed agreements are being established between the CVN 79 Program Office and platform GFE providers to provide a greater degree of control in management of on-time delivery of expected equipment, critical for avoiding shipbuilder disruption, and for control of cost.

FOR OFFICIAL USE ONLY

This document contains information EXEMPT FROM PUBLIC DISCLOSURE under FOIA Exemption 4 applies

16   Enclosure 2

c. **Stringent restrictions on change** – Changes from the CVN 78 baseline are being minimized to limit their disruption to the shipbuilder and the potential impact on cost. Where change is unavoidable, such as in the case of systems no longer being available due to obsolescence, a rigorous change control process is in place to fully explore alternatives and mitigate potential cost impacts. Where a GFE system change is proposed to provide additional capability to the ship, a disciplined resource and requirements review process at the senior Flag Officer level within the Pentagon is followed to thoroughly vet the proposed change.

The FORD Class aircraft carrier brings tremendous new capability to 21st century naval aviation with reduced manpower and sustainment requirements leading to a substantially reduced total ownership cost. This is in large part due to advanced government furnished systems incorporated in the design. As described in the preceding paragraphs, the Navy is focused on delivering these capabilities with costs reduced 5-10% in real terms from CVN 78.

COMPARISON TO CVN 77 AND CVN 78

After accounting for the $3.2B non-recurring cost to design the FORD Class aircraft carrier, the cost of the first of class CVN 78 is, in real terms, 18% more than the tenth NIMITZ Class aircraft carrier, the CVN 77, for a class of ship that will provide a 33% increase in warfighting capability, unmatched flexibility for future missions, and cost the taxpayer approximately $4B per ship less than a NIMITZ class carrier over its 50-year service life. Recognizing the responsibility to build aircraft carriers in the most affordable way possible, the Navy and shipbuilder have taken the actions described in this report to drive down the construction cost for CVN 79. These actions are expected to reduce the material costs for CVN 79 by 10-20% in real terms from CVN 78, and to reduce the man-hours required to build the CVN 79 by 15-25% from CVN 78. The man-hours required to build CVN 79, the second ship of the FORD Class, are expected to be 5-10% less than those required to build CVN 77.

Conclusion

The Navy and HII-NNS have made fundamental changes in the manner in which the JOHN F KENNEDY (CVN 79) will be built to eliminate the key roadblocks that were realized and were the largest impacts to cost performance during the construction of CVN 78. Simply addressing lessons learned and working harder is not good enough. The approach to carrier construction has undergone an extensive affordability review. As described in this report, the Navy and HII-NNS are committed to making the fundamental changes necessary to drive down and stabilize aircraft carrier construction costs for CVN 79 and beyond.

FOR OFFICIAL USE ONLY

This document contains information EXEMPT FROM PUBLIC DISCLOSURE under FOIA
Exemption 4 applies

17   Enclosure 2

Appendix B. Refueling Complex Overhaul (RCOH) for *George Washington* (CVN-73)

An additional issue relating to aircraft carriers that has been raised by the Navy's proposed FY2015 budget concerns funding for the mid-life nuclear refueling overhaul of the aircraft carrier *George Washington* (CVN-73). This appendix presents background information and potential oversight questions for Congress relating to this issue.

To operate for a full 50-year life, existing Nimitz (CVN-68) class nuclear-powered carriers are given a mid-life nuclear refueling overhaul, called a refueling complex overhaul (RCOH), when they are 20 to 25 years old, which is when their original nuclear fuel core has been exhausted. The RCOH gives the ship a new nuclear fuel core sufficient to power the ship for the remainder of its 50-year life. The RCOH also involves a significant amount of other overhaul, repair, and modernization work on the ship. An RCOH requires about 44 months from contract award to delivery. RCOHs are funded through the Navy's shipbuilding account (the Shipbuilding and Conversion, Navy [SCN] appropriation account).

RCOHs are done primarily at Huntington Ingalls Industries/Newport News Shipbuilding (HII/NNS) in Newport News, VA, and form a significant part of HII/NNS's business base, along with construction of new nuclear-powered aircraft carriers and construction of new nuclear-powered submarines. RCOHs in recent years have been scheduled in a more or less heel-to-toe fashion at HII/NNS—when one RCOH is done, the next one is scheduled to begin soon thereafter. RCOHs are done in a particular dry dock at HII/NNS, so a carrier undergoing an RCOH in that dry dock must have its work finished and depart the dry dock before the following carrier can be moved into the dry dock for its RCOH.

The next carrier scheduled for an RCOH is the *George Washington* (CVN-73). The total estimated cost of the CVN-73 RCOH in the Navy's FY2014 budget submission was $4,738.2 million (i.e., about $4.7 billion).

Until the FY2015 budget submission, the CVN-73 RCOH was scheduled for FY2016. The CVN-73 RCOH received $12 million in advance procurement (AP) funding in FY2012, $69.9 million in AP funding in FY2013, and $245.8 million in AP funding in FY2014. Under the Navy's FY2014 budget submission, another $491.1 million in AP funding was projected for FY2015, and the balance of the RCOH's estimated cost of $4,738.2 million was to be provided in FY2016 and FY2017.

As part of its FY2015 budget submission, DOD removed funding for the CVN-73 RCOH from the FY2015-FY2019 Future Years Defense Plan (FYDP) and is proposing to defer the question of whether to proceed with the CVN-73 RCOH until next year, when Congress will consider the FY2016 defense budget. The Navy's proposed FY2015 budget includes about $46 million in funding in the Operation and Maintenance, Navy (OMN) appropriation account to defuel CVN-73. Defueling the ship (i.e., removing the original nuclear fuel core) is an initial step to be performed on the ship at NNS, regardless of whether the ship is to undergo an RCOH or be inactivated.

DOD and Navy officials state that if Congress provides an indication this year that it supports the defense spending levels in the FY2015-FY2019 FYDP, which are higher than those called for in the Budget Control Act of 2011 as amended, then the FYDP would be reformulated for FY2016 and subsequent years to include the roughly $7.0 billion in additional funding that would be needed over the FYDP to fund the CVN-73 RCOH and keep the ship and its associated carrier air wing in service.[38] Of this $7.0 billion in additional funding, $796.2 million would be required in FY2015.[39]

DOD and Navy officials state that if Congress does not provide an indication this year that it supports the defense spending levels in the FYDP, CVN-73 would instead be inactivated (i.e., permanently retired from service), and its associated air wing would be disestablished. Other things held equal, inactivating CVN-73 would reduce the Navy's carrier force to 10 ships for the next 25 years or so (i.e., the period of time that CVN-73 would have remained in service if it had received an RCOH).

The Navy states that, of the funding for the CVN-73 RCOH that was provided in FY2012 and FY2013, $20.6 million represent sunk costs that would not be recoverable if CVN-73 were not to receive an RCOH. The Navy states that this $20.6 million "primarily supported prime contractor and government initial planning efforts for the refueling overhaul as well as some initial modernization GFI [government-furnished information] development efforts."[40]

Navy officials state that deferring until next year the decision on whether to proceed with the CVN-73 RCOH would mean that the RCOH, if were to occur, would be delayed some number of months from the schedule shown in the Navy's FY2014 budget submission, and consequently would likely become an FY2017 action rather than an FY2016 action. Navy officials state that if the delay in the start of the RCOH were not more than a certain number of months, it would not cause a cascading delay in the schedule for the following RCOH (to be done on CVN-74), because there is currently some slack time on the back end of the CVN-73 RCOH period to absorb some delay in the CVN-73 RCOH without affecting the schedule for the CVN-74 RCOH.

10 U.S.C. 5062(b) states that "The naval combat forces of the Navy shall include not less than 11 operational aircraft carriers." The requirement as stated in this statute is not contingent on the DOD budget being at a certain level in coming years. To the contrary, the central purpose of 10 U.S.C. 5062(b) is to act as a mandate to the executive branch to support force of not less than 11 carriers in executive branch planning, regardless of budgetary or other circumstances. DOD has not, as part of its FY2015 budget submission, requested that 10 U.S.C. 5062(b) be amended or repealed.

Potential oversight questions for Congress include the following:

- Is DOD's proposal to treat the issue of whether to proceed with the CVN-73 RCOH (and consequently whether there are to be 10 or 11 carriers for the next 25

---

[38] The estimated total cost to perform the CVN-73 RCOH and retain the carrier and its associated air wing is about $8.1 billion. (This figure includes about $5.9 to perform the RCOH and keep the ship in service, about $1.4 billion to retain the air wing, and about $800 million for associated logistics, manpower, and training costs.) The FY2015-FY2019 FYDP currently includes about $1.1 billion to support the inactivation of CVN-73. Reprogramming this $1.1 billion in inactivation funding to support the RCOH would leave a requirement for about $7.0 billion in additional funding. Source: Navy information paper provided to CRS by Navy Office of Legislative Affairs on April 7, 2014.

[39] The total estimated requirement for FY2015 is $842.2 million. This figure includes the $46 million currently in the budget for the ship's defueling, leaving a net requirement of $796.2 million in additional funding for FY2015. Source: Navy information paper provided to CRS by Navy Office of Legislative Affairs on April 7, 2014.

[40] Source: Navy information paper dated March 13, 2014, and provided to CRS by the Navy Office of Legislative Affairs on April 17, 2014.

years or so) as a question to be decided next year, depending on indications of congressional support for a certain DOD budget level in coming years, consistent with 10 U.S.C. 5062(b)? Does DOD's proposal in effect treat the 11-carrier requirement in 10 U.S.C. 5062(b) as an optional matter rather than a mandate? If so, would this create a precedent for the executive branch to treat similar provisions in the U.S. Code as optional matters rather than mandates? For example, would it create a precedent for DOD, if it so desired, to begin treating as an optional matter the longstanding requirement in 10 U.S.C. 5063(a) that the Marine Corps "shall be so organized as to include not less than three combat divisions and three air wings, and such other land combat, aviation, and other services as may be organic therein?" If the executive branch were to begin treating statutory provisions like 10 U.S.C. 5062(b) as optional matters rather than mandates, what implications might this have for policy and program execution, and for Congress's power to legislatively establish policy and program goals?

- What would be the operational impact for the Navy of reducing the carrier force to 10 ships for the next 25 years or so (and also eliminating its associated carrier air wing)? What impact would it have on the Navy's ability to fulfill its missions?

- If the FDYP were reformulated to include the $7 billion in additional funding needed to keep CVN-73 and its associated air wing, what other defense programs would have their funding reduced, and what would be the impact of these reductions on DOD's ability to fulfill its missions?

- What would be the impact on HII/NNS and the other parts of the aircraft carrier industrial base if CVN-73 were inactivated rather than given an RCOH? What impact, if any, would this have on the cost of other work performed at NNS during these years, and on the eventual cost of the CVN-74 RCOH?[41]

Author Contact Information

Ronald O'Rourke
Specialist in Naval Affairs
rorourke@crs.loc.gov, 7-7610

---

[41] For press reports discussing the industrial-base aspects of the issue, see Lara Seligman, "Shipbuilder: Navy's Timeline For CVN-73 'Not In Accordance With Our Plan,'" *Inside the Navy*, March 24, 2014; Olga Belogolova, "PEO Carriers: A Cut From 11 To 10 Carriers Would Impact Industrial Base," *Inside the Navy*, February 24, 2014; Michael Fabey, "Foregoing Carrier RCOH Won't Disrupt Future Work, HII CEO Says," *Aerospace Daily & Defense Report*, March 25, 2014: 4; Rick Giannini and Darrell Grow, "Why Aircraft Carrier Workers Deserve a Better Plan from the Pentagon," *Defense One (www.defenseone.com)*, March 23, 2014.